# VANISHING ANIMALS

## *Preserving Nature's Rarities*

\*

### PHILIP STREET

### THE SCIENTIFIC BOOK CLUB

121 Charing Cross Road

London W.C.2

*First published in mcmlxi
by Faber and Faber Limited*

*Printed in Great Britain by
Latimer Trend & Co Ltd Plymouth*

Dedicated
with good wishes to my friend
MARY THOMSON

# Contents

*

# The Problem of Fauna Preservation

*

The preservation of the remaining animal life of the world, and especially of those species which are already approaching extinction, is the most urgent problem facing zoologists and naturalists everywhere today. Until the end of the nineteenth century no one seemed to care whether animal species survived or not, and the fact that many managed to linger on into the present century was a matter of sheer luck, and certainly not in any way due to conscious attempts at preservation by man. But with the turn of the century came a change in the climate of opinion. Indiscriminate destruction of wildlife became unpopular in many quarters, and increasing efforts began to be made by influential groups of people determined to do all they could to stem the alarming rate at which animals and species had been disappearing for ever during the preceding century. For the past sixty years, and particularly over the last two or three decades, the general public has become increasingly aware of its own responsibilities for demanding that threatened species shall be accorded adequate protection against the selfish interests of ruthless exploitation and the results of ignorance and indifference.

Today greater efforts are being made than ever before to ensure that no more animal species are allowed to vanish from the earth. Preservation societies and similar bodies have been founded in many countries, and their efforts are now co-ordinated by the International Union for the Conservation of Nature. Enlightened propaganda is enlisting increasing support for this work both from Governments and from the public.

There is, however, no single reason why certain animals are rare today, and there is no single solution to the problem of their preservation. Many species owe their present precarious position to man's activities. Some he slaughtered ruthlessly because they were economically valuable to him, while others he nearly exterminated in the interests of so-called sport. Many of them were incredibly abundant in earlier times, but were nevertheless reduced to the very verge of extinction without apparently stimulating any feelings of regret. Other species suffered at the hands of the collector, who sometimes collected the animals themselves and sometimes their eggs.

As civilization spread and more and more acres of virgin forest or scrub were cleared to make way for increased agricultural production, so the area available for wildlife steadily decreased, and with it the total animal population it could support. Man in his travels, too, was liable to introduce, either by design or by accident, alien species into many lands, and these sometimes caused havoc among the indigenous fauna, destroying many species and endangering the future existence of others. Besides the many species which have thus become rare today through man's intervention, there are others which were rare when they were first discovered, and even without man's assistance they would probably not have survived for very much longer.

There are three main methods by which animals can be preserved. Some can be saved by sufficiently rigid protection in their native habitats, combined with controlled exploitation in the case of those species which are commercially important. Other animals must inevitably suffer banishment from large parts of their original range in cases where their requirements are in conflict with the requirements of an expanding agriculture developed to supply the needs of a growing population striving towards a higher standard of living. The best hope for these is that they may be able to maintain sufficient numbers in special nature reserves or national parks where they can thrive unmolested by farmer, sportsman or poacher.

A third group of rare animals consists of those which have already become virtually or completely extinct in the wild state. For them, continued survival must depend upon the establishment and maintenance of as many small breeding stocks as possible in zoos and zoological parks in various parts of the world. As civilization and exploitation continue to make inroads into the wild life of the world the number of species which will eventually have to be maintained in captivity is likely to increase. For this reason the steady improvement in our knowledge of the keeping and breeding of wild animals in captivity is of great importance to the future of fauna preservation.

Since this book is about fauna preservation it will be mainly concerned with species which have been brought to the verge of extinction and have then been saved. But lest the many examples of preservation which will be dealt with in subsequent chapters should give the idea that all species in danger are ultimately saved, we might look at some species which were not so fortunate. The rate of extinction has certainly increased in the past 150 years or so. Since 1800 no fewer than 44 species of mammals alone have become extinct and the number of birds which have suffered a similar fate is probably much in excess of this figure.

The classic example of extinction in modern times is that of the passenger pigeon. On 1st September 1914 the last survivor of the species, a hen bird called Martha, died in the Cincinnati Zoological Gardens. Martha's death signalled the end of one of the most remarkable stories of mass destruction in the history of animal life. In its heyday a century earlier the passenger pigeon had existed in such vast numbers that the very possibility of its ever becoming extinct must have been unthinkable. Nevertheless through man's thoughtless destruction it was wiped off the face of the earth for ever.

Accounts of the immense flocks of passenger pigeons encountered in earlier times all over the North American continent would be difficult to believe had they not been written by distinguished naturalists whose integrity was beyond doubt. Audubon, the great American ornithologist, estimated one such flight which he witnessed to contain well over one thousand million birds. The birds passed over him for hours on end in such concentration that the sunlight was almost blotted out. In all directions as far as the eye could see the sky was filled with pigeons, layer upon layer of them, and all flying at speeds approaching sixty miles an hour.

Another leading ornithologist, Alexander Wilson, estimated that a flock which he encountered in 1832 contained well over two thousand million birds. The flight of this flock was more than a mile wide, and took four hours to pass him at top speed, which means its length must have been something like 240 miles!

The amount of food that these travelling flocks would consume must have been enormous. Allowing only an ounce for each pigeon, which is surely an underestimate, Wilson's flock would require 30,000 tons of food each day. In fact we are told that they were great gluttons, sometimes feeding until their crops actually burst. Their food consisted in the main of all kinds of nuts, seeds and fruits.

It is difficult for us to visualize such immense numbers of birds. The total bird population of the British Isles has been estimated at about two hundred million birds. So Audubon's single flock of pigeons contained at least five times as many birds as the total number of birds in Britain, and Wilson's flock was twice this size.

The nesting of the passenger pigeon was just as fantastic as its mass flights. A flock would take over a whole forest, and for several hundred square miles there was not a tree without a nest. A hundred and more nests in a single tree was a common occurrence. So great was the weight of these nests and their growing nestlings that quite big branches were broken off, and at the end of the nesting season the forest looked as though it had stood in the path of a tornado. The floor would be covered inches deep in droppings, and all the grass and undergrowth killed, as well as many of the trees. It took years for the forest to recover from one use as a nesting site.

The passenger pigeon was quite safe until the white settlers appeared in America. The Indians killed a certain number for food with bow and arrow but they were wise enough in the ways of wild life to refrain from any killing during the nesting season. But the white man, in America as in other parts of the world, slaughtered without thought for the future consequences.

To the white settlers, though, and especially to those pioneers who pushed the trail westwards, the passenger pigeon was a godsend. They were good to eat, and they were always available even when other food was extremely scarce. As a result large numbers were killed. Even so it is doubtful whether the settlers themselves would have seriously depleted the pigeon populations.

With the coming of the railroad, however, came also the professional pigeon killer, who discovered that huge profits could be made out of pigeons sent back by rail to the large towns. His task was an easy one. Living as they did in such concentrations, killing the pigeons was absurdly easy. Various methods were used, and in the 1860's, which was the boom period for pigeon killing, a man could earn up to £10 a day, and £10 was worth something in those days.

Firing at a flock on the wings with both barrels of a shotgun often brought down well over 100 birds, and as many as 3,000 roosting birds could be trapped in a skilfully laid net. Sometimes the flocks flew so low that large numbers could be knocked down with a pole, and even boatmen were known to bring them down with their oars.

How many pigeons there were in North America before the great slaughter began no one knows. But however great the population it could never stand the annual slaughter of tens of millions such as occurred in the 1860's and 1870's. By the 1880's it was becoming clear to a few enlightened minds that unless a halt was called the passenger pigeon would be annihilated. Their warnings, however, went unheeded, so that by 1900 it was all but extinct, and the few remaining wild specimens disappeared within the next few years.

Among those who had foreseen the doom of the passenger pigeon were the Cincinnati Zoological Gardens. In 1879 they bought a few pairs in the hope that they might be able to keep the species going if it became extinct in the wild state. It was a vain hope, however, for the birds did not thrive in captivity, and few young ones were reared. One by one they died off until only Martha, hatched in 1885, remained.

When she finally died on that September afternoon in 1914 elaborate precautions were taken to preserve her body for the Smithsonian Institute in Washington, to whom she had been promised. The moment she was dead she was rushed off to the Cincinnati Ice Company, who froze her body for shipment to Washington. Today she is on public exhibition in the U.S. National Museum, a permanent reminder of the devastation that thoughtless man can bring to the animal life of the world.

The passenger pigeon may be the most spectacular example of extermination in modern times, but the most famous is the case of the dodo. This curious bird has indeed become the symbol of extinction. It was first discovered on the island of Mauritius by the Dutch Admiral Van Neck in 1598, but the description which he brought home of the dodo was disbelieved by the naturalists of his time, and indeed it must have sounded a most improbable bird. Today we know that his account was substantially correct, and that the dodo was indeed an improbable bird.

A member of the pigeon family, it was nevertheless larger than a turkey, very heavily built with a pair of almost absurdly short, stout legs. It had a large hooked beak and a short curly tail, but the feature which was to prove its undoing was its complete inability to fly, its wings being mere rudiments. It was thus completely without defence, though before Mauritius was discovered by European sailors this was not a disadvantage, because no animals large enough to prey on it existed on the island. From 1598 the dodo was systematically reduced in numbers by sailors who called in at the island, but its final doom probably dates from 1644, when the island was first colonized by the Dutch. With them they brought dogs and pigs, and some of these escaped and established feral populations in the woods where the dodo lived. Both animals would prey on the eggs and young of the dodo, and even perhaps on the adult birds. From this time its extermination must have been rapid. When the process was finally completed we do not know, but we do know that by 1693 the bird had finally disappeared from the island which had been its only home. On the neighbouring island of Rodriguez there lived another large member of the pigeon family, the solitaire. This bird was similar in size to the dodo, but had longer legs and a longer neck. When Leguat, the French navigator, visited Rodriguez in 1691, he discovered the bird and left a description of its appearance and habits, as well as a drawing. The reasons for its disappearance by 1761 were probably similar to those for the dodo.

More recent times have seen the extermination of another large flight-less bird, the great auk. This was the largest member of the auk tribe, to which the guillemots, razorbills and puffins belong. Like them it was a bird of the temperate and arctic regions of the northern hemisphere, occurring in widely separated areas in the North Atlantic from America to Europe. Its main populations, however, were centred on a few small rocky islands near Iceland, called the Garefowl Skerries, garefowl being the common name for the birds, and Funk Island off the Newfoundland coast. From the time of their discovery in 1534 until the last pair was killed in 1844, the garefowl were subject to continuous persecution. Ship's crews would spend the whole summer on Funk Island killing them for the sake of their feathers. Stone pens were constructed, and into these the birds were driven like sheep, their bodies apparently being left to rot. Why the garefowl feathers were considered worth all this trouble is not clear.

Of the mammals which have become extinct in recent times through man's activities perhaps the most publicized has been the quagga. This was the most southerly of the various species of zebra in South Africa. The zebras show considerable variation in their striping, and the quagga was less completely striped than any of the other species, the striping being confined to its front end, though the extent of the striping along the back apparently varied considerably from individual to individual. When the Dutch first came to South Africa the quaggas existed in vast herds, which associated with equally large concentrations of white-tailed gnu and ostriches, the three species grazing together in complete harmony. This association between the three species was probably advantageous to each of them. The senses of sight, scent and hearing were probably developed to different extents in the three animals, so the mixed herds would benefit by a kind of pooling of abilities. The ostriches, for example, because of their height and very keen vision, would be able to warn of the approach of man or lions long before the other two species would have been able to detect the danger. The quaggas, on the other hand, would probably have had a more acute sense of smell than the ostriches and the gnus. Fear in herding animals is extremely infectious, and if one species showed anxiety it would quickly spread to the others.

From the time of their arrival the Boers exploited the quaggas, using the meat to feed their native workers and the hides to make sacks for storing grain and leather for their shoes. In 1800 the quaggas are described as existing in droves consisting of countless thousands, but by 1840 they had already been exterminated over a large part of their original range. Much reduced populations existed only in Cape Colony and to the north of the Orange River, and the persecution of these remaining herds continued. In 1850 the last two quaggas in Cape Colony were killed on the Tygerberg Mountain. In the Orange Free State, however, the quagga managed to hold on for another twenty or more years, but the last one is believed to have been shot in 1878. A few specimens had been caught and sent to zoos, and one of these, which died in Amsterdam Zoo on 12th September 1883, was the very last survivor of the species. During the eighty odd years which have elapsed since the quagga became extinct in the wild state occasional reports have been received that quaggas have been seen in South West Africa, but the species has never reappeared. The most likely explanation of the reports is that there has been confusion with Hartmann's zebra which lives in this area and might be confused with the quagga when seen from a distance.

As the nineteenth century progressed all the zebra species of Africa suffered increasing persecution. The quagga bore the initial brunt of the white man's arrival because, being the most southerly species, it was the first to come into contact with him. North of the Orange River similiar enormous herds of Burchell's zebra lived on the plains. These plains were colonized about a quarter of a century later than the plains on which the quagga lived, and thus it was that Burchell's zebra was exterminated correspondingly later. It might well have been saved had a timely warning been heeded. In 1885 a suggestion was made that it might be used for draught purposes, and a strong plea for its complete protection to save it from extinction was included in the report. Nothing, however, was done about this, so that by about 1900 the species had become extinct. The last to go was a single specimen which died at London Zoo in 1909.

Fauna preservation is much more than a series of declarations that this or that animal shall be accorded complete protection. It is in fact an ecological problem concerned with the conservation of wildlife as a whole, with particular emphasis on species which are in danger of extermination, or might become so in the future. There have been many examples of man upsetting the balance of nature, either consciously or accidentally, and in consequence endangering species which previously were quite able to hold their own. One of the important ways in which he has interfered with this balance has been the introduction of alien species, which have then either preyed upon native species, or have competed successfully with them for available supplies of food.

One of the most instructive examples of the perils of introducing alien species was the now classic case of the release of the mongoose in Jamaica to combat the rat menace in the 1870's. As in so many other parts of the world, the black and brown rats were introduced to Jamaica from Europe by ships trading with the island. Here they thrived and became the greatest menace to the sugar-cane planter. Enormous sums were spent on rat killing, but still up to 20 per cent of the total crop was being destroyed by rats a century ago. Several unsuccessful attempts were made to introduce animals which it was hoped might prey upon the rats. In 1844 a number of specimens of the giant neotropical toad were introduced, and before long a large population had developed. These large toads had the reputation of feeding upon young rats, but whether they did so in Jamaica or not, their efforts were insufficient, and the rats continued to increase. Ferrets were also tried, and these might have been more successful, but unfortunately they were themselves attacked by insect parasites which they were unable to cope with.

The next idea was to import and turn loose specimens of Indian mongoose. These animals were known to be sworn enemies of the rat, and it was felt that they might succeed where other animals had failed. Accordingly in 1872 considerable numbers were imported by several sugar estates. They were not, however, wild specimens from India, but had been bred in captivity in London, where they had presumably never seen a rat. They proved a complete failure, and far from attacking the rats they were obviously afraid of them. In the same year, however, one estate imported four males and five females direct from India, and these showed all the aggressiveness towards the rats that had been expected. They thrived, and before long the mongoose was common throughout the island, and the rats were fast disappearing.

Unfortunately, however, they did their job only too well, and it was not long before there were insufficient rats to maintain the rapidly growing mongoose population. So they turned their attention to the other wildlife of the island. With their fondness for eggs, it was the reptiles and ground-nesting birds which bore the brunt of the mongoose attacks, and many species were exterminated. Had it been possible the mongoose itself would have been eliminated, but the best that could be achieved was to keep its numbers down to reasonable limits at a considerable annual cost. It is now firmly established as a member of the fauna of Jamaica, representing rather a poor exchange for the many species which have been lost for ever.

Introductions made by man have played an important part in reducing the fauna of Australia and New Zealand. In both countries rats and cats have caused great damage, and in Australia the native fauna has also had to contend with the feral dingo. Rats, cats, dogs and pigs have, in fact, played a leading part in altering the character of the fauna in many parts of the world. Many times it has been shown that it is easier to introduce an alien species without considering the possible consequences of the introduction than it is to eliminate it when its disadvantages have been revealed.

One of the most important considerations in maintaining the balance of nature is the relationship between predators and prey. In a completely natural population these two kinds of animals maintain a steady balance, and to disturb it is to risk the wholesale destruction of the very species it has been designed to save. One of the classic examples, which should have served as a warning, was the policy initiated by President Theodore Roosevelt in the early years of this century on the Kaibab plateau in North America. Here the deer herds were given absolute protection, while at the same time the puma and the wolf, the natural enemies of the deer, were destroyed under the mistaken impression that this would help in the preservation of the deer. What actually happened was that the deer, suddenly relieved of all enemies, both animal and human, proceeded to increase so rapidly that in a short time they were overgrazing their territory. Within a few years what had once been fertile grassland was being changed to desert, so reducing the available amount of food that thousands of deer died of starvation. There are plenty of more recent examples of a similar disregard for the importance of maintaining a predator-prey balance. Thus, again in America, the prairie marmot is trapped because it destroys the pasture on the cattle ranges, while at the same time its chief enemy the coyote, which would play a major part in keeping its numbers in check, is also destroyed. In Britain, too, war is waged on rats and mice, and also on the stoats and weasels which are their natural enemies.

One of the most important demonstrations of the danger of destroying natural predators has been seen in arctic Canada. Here from the earliest times the caribou, the wild form of the reindeer, has been of great economic importance to the Eskimo. Its only important natural enemy is the wolf, and in an attempt to increase the caribou populations a campaign was conducted against the wolf. The result, though, was quite unexpected. Instead of the caribou herds increasing steadily in numbers, after a few years they began to be seriously depleted, and the reasons for this were directly connected with the reduction of the wolf populations.

During the summer months food for the caribou is always plentiful, and they eat great quantities, much of which becomes converted into a considerable layer of fat. During the winter this fat is gradually used up to keep the animals going. For the rest they rely upon the lichens which they are able to dig out from the snow. Until man tried to interfere with the population balance between the wolves and the caribou, the numbers of the latter were kept in check by the wolves. As soon as the number of wolves were seriously reduced, however, they were no longer able to keep the number of caribou steady, with the result that they increased quite rapidly. More caribou meant increased winter grazing on the rather limited stocks of lichen, and this soon resulted in the total quantity of lichen being reduced, so that an increasing number of caribou were trying to exist on a steadily decreasing amount of lichen, with the result of course that great numbers died of starvation, and the general condition of the remainder deteriorated. Out of this experience has grown the realization that in order to preserve the caribou herds it is equally important to preserve their natural enemies the wolves.

Another interesting and important aspect of the balance of nature has been revealed in the Kruger National Park in South Africa since the war. About ten years ago it was realized that although elephants and buffalo were steadily increasing in number in the Park, many of the smaller antelopes were decreasing rapidly. As a result of a careful consideration of the position the view was put forward that this serious depletion in the populations of many of the Park's species could be traced to a decree which forbade grass burning. For hundreds, perhaps thousands, of years, grass burning to encourage the growth of tender new shoots, had been practised over large areas of Africa, including the Kruger region. The Kruger authorities banned this traditional procedure on the grounds that grass burning represented an interference with nature.

It has, however, been pointed out that grass burning is of such long standing that it does in fact represent part of the natural sequence of events. That so many animals and so many species could be seen in so many areas of Africa in earlier times might well have been due in part to this traditional grass burning which would ensure a continuous supply of fresh young grass for them to eat. Strong circumstantial evidence in favour of this conclusion is that if landowners in areas surrounding the Kruger want to entice the smaller game from the Park on to their land, they burn large areas of their own grass. The new blades which appear a few weeks afterwards prove an irresistible attraction, and the antelopes cross the Park boundaries in force.

Another problem facing areas where the animal life is completely protected is the possibility that the predators may become too numerous for the available prey. This is particularly liable to occur where predators were killed to a relatively greater extent than their prey in the days before protection. In every national park a careful watch must be kept on the predator-prey balance, and a certain number of predators shot if it seems they are getting too numerous for the available prey.

One of the most difficult problems facing those concerned with wildlife preservation in Africa is the tremendous toll taken by poachers. In many places poaching is not merely a matter of the odd individual taking an occasional antelope, but a highly organized business. Some poaching is done actually within the boundaries of the national parks, but much more common and less risky for those who indulge in it is poaching outside the park boundaries. During the dry season the game may well have to travel outside the limits of the parks to the remaining water holes, and it is then that they become easy prey for the unscrupulous.

In large-scale poaching bush fences are built, often several miles long, across the known routes which the animals take on their journeys from the park to the water. Gaps are left in these fences, and each gap is carefully snared. When the animals are caught they are generally cut up on the spot, and the meat carried away to be sold. The skins are usually left around for the hyaenas to clear up, because to be caught with them would be too incriminating. There is a great deal of waste, since a considerable proportion of the animals caught in this way are never collected. With such vast areas to patrol the game wardens find it difficult enough to track down poachers within the parks. To pursue them beyond the boundaries and bring them to justice is virtually impossible except in a minority of cases. The native poacher, too, is often a desperate character who is well armed, and would rather commit murder than be caught.

In recent years considerable concern has been expressed about large-scale slaughter of game in Southern Rhodesia in the interests of tsetse-fly control. In 1948, for example, no fewer than 22,100 animals were destroyed, including more than 11,000 antelopes. This slaughter has been going on since 1924 and during this period more than half a million animals are known to have been shot. In recent years doubts have been cast upon the possibility of controlling the tsetse fly by this method. It would be a tragedy if practically all the wild life of Rhodesia were to be wiped out to no effective purpose.

The modern popularity of spear fishing has also brought anxieties about its ultimate effective on inshore fish populations in areas where the sport is practised on a large scale. In a short space of ten years the coastal waters of considerable parts of the

## The Problem of Fauna Preservation

Mediterranean, of many West Indian islands, and of the warmer parts of America, have been practically denuded of rock fish. Unless some legislation can be effected quickly it seems certain that many species of fish are doomed to final extinction within a comparatively short time. The modern spring-loaded speargun, with its range of thirty feet or more, is indeed a lethal weapon, and tens of thousands of these are sold every year to spear fishing enthusiasts. Disquieting reports of the achievements of these sportsmen continue to come in. As an example we may take the case of the champion spear fisherman of the Balearic Islands, whose proud claim it is to have practically annihilated all the larger fish around one of the islands in the space of ten years.

The most encouraging fact concerning the future of the animal life of the world today is that everywhere there are bodies concerned with preservation and conservation, and that they are steadily gaining public support for their work. We will end this chapter by looking at the more important of these bodies, and the way in which they work. One of the first, and still one of the most influential societies concerned with preservation is the Fauna Preservation Society. This was formed as far back as 1903 in London as the Society for the Preservation of the Fauna of the Empire. In 1950 it changed its name to the Fauna Preservation Society.

The most important modern development was the foundation in 1948 of the International Union for the Protection of Nature, afterwards renamed the Union for the Conservation of Nature and Natural Resources. Its purpose was to co-ordinate the work of preservation societies all over the world, and to keep a careful watch on the progress of any species threatened with extinction. Where necessary advice would be offered to Governments as to the best way of conserving their wildlife, and campaigns conducted where it was felt that insufficient care was being taken of a rare or diminishing species. In August 1949 a

## The Problem of Fauna Preservation

Survival Service of the Union was inaugurated, with a four-point programme. The first task was to collect all the available information about threatened species, and the second to verify this information by sending out a questionnaire to persons living in the areas where the threatened species lived. This questionnaire was very full, and asked about the past and present range of the animals, about any changes in their habits, the causes leading to their decrease, and asked for suggestions as to what measures might be taken to ensure their survival. In this way much valuable information was collected. The third function of the Survival Service was to distribute this information as widely as possible. Once all these things had been done for any threatened species the Service would be in a position to advise and assist governments and other organizations in their efforts to conserve it.

One of the first things the Survival Service did was to draw up a list of gravely endangered species which needed the special attention of the Service. Periodically this list is revised. Some species which have responded favourably to protection are removed from it, and others whose status has deteriorated are added. It would be difficult to overestimate the value of the publicity which a threatened species gets by being placed on this list. The first list, drawn up in 1949, contained 13 birds and 14 mammals.

In September 1958 the responsibilities of the International Union were further extended by the establishment of an International Committee on National Parks. Its purpose is to strengthen international co-operation in matters relating to reserves and national parks throughout the world, to serve as an information centre on reserves and parks, to advise on national park systems and to undertake scientific research.

Since the early months of 1959 the most urgent conservation operation ever attempted has been in progress. In December 1958 the great dam across the Zambesi River at Kariba was finally completed and sealed, and the waters behind it gradually began to rise. Not until early in 1963 is it expected that the vast lake which is being formed will be completely filled. When this does at last occur it will be by far the largest artificial lake in the world, with an area of no less than 2,500 square miles. As the waters rose the high ground and the hills would become cut off as islands, and on these islands many animals would be trapped by the rising waters.

Because of its rich vegetation and the abundance of shelter and water, the Zambesi valley has always supported a rich fauna, and was also an important migration highway between the dry country to the west and Portuguese East Africa. Before the dam was finally sealed it was clear that enormous numbers of animals would be trapped on the high ground as the waters rose, and the Southern Rhodesian Game Department had already recruited four rangers with two boats to conduct rescue work by the beginning of 1958. By February 1959 Operation Noah, as the rescue work was popularly called, had already rescued more than 300 animals and had released them on the dry ground beyond the edge of the lake.

By this time, however, it was becoming obvious that the measures so far proposed were quite inadequate to deal with the problem when it reached its peak. The boundary between Northern and Southern Rhodesia ran through the middle of the new lake. Southern Rhodesia was doing something to solve the problem, though a much greater effort would be required to be really effective, but Northern Rhodesia seemed prepared to do nothing to help. By early March it seemed increasingly doubtful whether the Northern Government would be prepared to do anything effective, so the Northern Rhodesian Game Preservation and Hunting Association decided to appeal to the Fauna Preservation Society for help. The response was immediate, and a press conference was arranged in London on March 19th. As a result of this the plight of the animals was featured in many newspapers and magazines, and a public appeal was launched by the Fauna Preservation Society for funds to buy boats and equipment.

As a result of these and other efforts the task of rescuing the trapped animals became much more effective. Today the rescue operations continue in full swing and are likely to do so until early in 1963, when it is calculated the lake will have reached its final limits. Lt.-Col. R. A. Critchley, the President of the Game Preservation and Hunting Association of Northern Rhodesia, wrote a progress report on Operation Noah in *Oryx* in December 1959. One paragraph in his report is significant because it gives some idea of the value of properly organized preservation bodies, and also of the value of mobilizing public opinion. 'There is no doubt,' he wrote, 'that public opinion, and the efforts of the Fauna Preservation Society, have been a major factor in persuading both the Northern and Southern Rhodesian Governments to treat Operation Noah seriously. Without this help and the support of the Press there was always a danger of animal rescue at Kariba being regarded as mere sentimental nonsense. The public of the Federation was never so game conscious as it is now, and the tragedy of Kariba may help in the future to focus public attention on the many other game conservation problems which are waiting to be solved in this part of Africa.'

So successful were the initial efforts, despite the handicap of insufficient funds and equipment, that already by the end of July 1959 nearly 1,900 mammals had been rescued from the islands and released on the mainland. As far as possible the animals are taken to game reserves, where of course they will stand the best chance of survival. One interesting fact has emerged from the rescue work. When mammals are captured it has been found that their temperatures rise, sometimes quite considerably, especially with very nervous species like impala. If these are released directly on the mainland they lie exhausted for some time while their temperatures fall to normal. So they are put into the water a short distance from the shore, the immersion bringing down their temperatures to normal by the time they have reached dry land.

## 2

# Controlled Exploitation—
# A Population Problem

*

Indiscriminate exploitation of economically valuable animals has been an important cause bringing animals to verge of extinction. Their preservation poses a special kind of problem for the conservationist. To expect that all exploitation shall be abandoned is quite unrealistic, since man does rely to a considerable extent upon the natural resources provided by the animal kingdom. The practical solution to the problem lies in discovering the extent to which any population can be exploited without endangering its survival, and this can only be done after exhaustive investigations into the factors which control its population numbers.

For the past sixty years a great deal of research has been done into the factors controlling the populations of many of our food fishes, much of it in connection with the overfishing problem, and the methods used will give valuable clues to the methods which will have to be adopted before the permissible extent of the exploitation of any animal can be determined. Similar experimental information, though less extensive, has been collected for whales and some populations of seals.

Until the end of the nineteenth century it was not generally believed that fishing fleets could catch enough fish to produce any measurable effect on the numbers of fish in the sea. By then, however, the combined effects of the introduction of the otter

## Controlled Exploitation—A Population Problem

trawl in the 1880's and the increase in the size and numbers of the fishing vessels as steam replaced sail were beginning to show. There were now clear indications that the stocks of fish on some at least of the fishing grounds were becoming depleted. Since this first recognition of the existence of an overfishing problem, the diminishing stocks of fish on many of the principal fishing grounds have been a constant source of anxiety to everyone connected with the fishing industry. Fishery scientists have made detailed studies of the effects of fishing on fish populations, in the belief that only with such knowledge can a satisfactory solution of the problem be worked out. The results of their work, one of the biggest single contributions made to our knowledge of animal populations, contain much that is of interest to the conservationist.

Long before the possibility of overfishing became generally recognized, one or two authorities had considered the likely effects of the steady increase in the rate of fishing that was taking place throughout the nineteenth century, and had concluded that a state of overfishing was already in being. From the available evidence it seems fairly clear that these earlier investigators were rather premature in their conclusions. Although their analyses of the final effects of a continually increasing rate of fishing proved ultimately correct, an actual state of overfishing did not occur to any serious extent until some decades after they were writing.

One of the earliest references to overfishing occurs in the *Guide to the Fishmarket*, written by Dr. Bellamy, a Cornishman, as long ago as 1842. 'Fishing, taken generally,' wrote Dr. Bellamy, 'interferes in the slightest way with the habits of the creatures in question; but the employment of a trawl, during a long series of years, must assuredly act with the greatest prejudice towards them. Dragged along with force over considerable areas of marine bottom, it tears away, promiscuously, hosts of the inferior beings there resident, besides bringing destruc-

34

tion on the multitudes of smaller fishes, the whole of which, be it observed, are the appointed diet of those edible species sought as human food. It also disturbs and drags forth the masses of deposited ova of various species. An interference with the economical arrangement of creation, of such magnitude and of such long duration, will hereafter bring its fruits in a perceptible dimunition of these articles of consumption for which we have so great necessity. The trawl is already fast bringing ruin on numbers of the poorer orders requiring the most considerable attention.'

In the light of modern knowledge we know much of what Dr. Bellamy wrote to be true. He was in error, though, about the destruction of fish eggs. These are found not on the sea bed, but floating among the plankton near the surface, immune from the destructive advance of the trawl. Only the herring among our important food fishes fixes its eggs to the sea bed, but since it chooses stony weed-free ground not frequented by other fish, except at times the haddock, they, too, in the main, escape destruction by the trawls.

If we turn to James Bertram's *Harvest of the Sea* we find that he, writing twenty-two years later, also had much to say about overfishing. In particular he was convinced that for some time haddock stocks had been steadily decreasing. In reply to the question, 'Where are the haddocks?' which he put to a Newhaven fisherman, he received the reply, 'They are about all eaten up, sir.' He then goes on, 'and I believe this to be true. The shore races of that fish have long disappeared, and our fishermen have now to seek this most palatable inhabitant of the sea afar off in the deep waters. Vast numbers of the haddock used to be taken in the Firth of Forth, but during late years they have become very scarce, and the boats now require to go a night's voyage to seek for them. If we knew the minutiae of the life of this fish, we should be better able to regulate the season for its capture, and the percentage that we might with safety take from the water without deteriorating the breeding power of the animal.' This last sentence is particularly interesting because it is one of the first occasions on which the idea of controlled exploitation was put forward.

In a later chapter he returns to the decrease of haddock stocks, contrasting the normal yearly fluctuations in abundance, characteristic of all fish populations, with a continual steady decrease. 'Although there have been from time to time sudden disappearances of the haddock from particular fishing grounds, as indeed there have been of all fish, that is a different, a totally different matter from what the fisher folk and the public have now to complain of—viz.: a yearly decreasing supply. Mr. Griere, of the Café Royal, Edinburgh, tells me that this season (August 1865) he is paying ninepence each for these fish, and is very glad to get them even at that price. I took part in a newspaper controversy about the scarcity of the haddock, and I found plenty of opponents ready to maintain that there was no scarcity, but that any quantity could be captured. In some degree that is the truth, but what is the hook-power required now to capture "any quantity", and how long does it take to obtain a given number, as compared with former times, when 'hat fish was supposed to be more plentiful? Why do we require for instance, to send to Norway and other distant places for haddocks and other white fish? The only answer I can give is that we cannot get enough at home.'

Whether or not Bertram was justified, on such information as was available, in regarding the existence of overfishing as proved is not really important. What is significant is that he sees the problem in its modern form. As we shall find, the weight of fish caught for a given effort is a much more reliable guide to the existence and degree of overfishing than the total landings.

Bellamy and Bertram may have been rather premature in their conclusions, but it was not very long before the fishermen themselves were showing increasing concern about the stocks of fish in the North Sea. As a result a Royal Commission was set up to examine the state of the fishing industry. Michael Graham, in his book *The Fish Gate*, quotes some of the fishermen's evidence before this Commission. This brings out clearly the fact that whereas the fishermen stressed the continual reduction in the weight of fish caught by each vessel, some members of the Commission attached more importance to the fact that the total weight of fish caught on the grounds was being maintained, apparently not realizing the significance of the fact that this was achieved only by using a steadily increasing number of vessels, with continually improving gear. In consequence the Commission was unconvinced, and in its report merely stated: 'It is alleged that although there may be an increase in the total amount of fish brought to market, the takes of each boat are smaller, in spite of the improved fishing gear, and that fish are really scarcer than formerly. To decide what amount of truth there is in this view of the case is, in the present state of our knowledge, impossible.'

In the same year, such was the uncertainty of opinion on the subject of overfishing that Thomas Henry Huxley, in his inaugural address to the International Fisheries Exhibition, was able to express his opinion that 'the cod fishery, the herring fishery, the pilchard fishery, the mackerel fishery, and probably all the great sea fisheries, are inexhaustible; that is to say, that nothing we do seriously affects the number of fish. And any attempt to regulate these fisheries seems consequently, from the nature of the case, to be useless.'

Ten years later, however, increased evidence of overfishing was recognized by a Select Committee of the House of Commons, which reported: 'but when we turn to the great fishing grounds of the North Sea, if your Committee is to rely on the evidence which has been laid before them by all persons interested in the fisheries, whether trawlers or linesmen, whether smack-owners or fishermen, whether scientific experts or statisticians, there seems to be no doubt that a considerable diminution has occurred amongst the more valuable classes of flat fish, especially among soles and plaice. It is true that there will not be found a great falling off in the bulk of these fishes landed on the east coast. But the appliances for catching them have of recent years been greatly increased in size and efficiency, and the fishing grounds have been largely extended in the area, trawlers going as far as the coast of Iceland to the north, and to the Portuguese coast to the south. The great falling off too in the size of the flat fish caught on the older grounds in the North Sea is also a matter of universal observation.'

From then on the existence of overfishing becomes more and more evident to everyone concerned with the fishing industry, and today we have an abundance of facts and figures relating to the last fifty years or so and indicating beyond doubt that during this period overfishing on many fishing grounds, especially those in the North Sea, has become progressively more acute.

The onset and increase of overfishing make it increasingly difficult to catch fish, and this is reflected in the figures for the amount of fish landed per day's absence from port. Such figures are available from the early days of this century, and tell us a great deal about the stocks of fish on the various fishing grounds. In 1906 English steam trawlers fishing in the North Sea landed an average of 17·6 cwt. of fish for each day's absence. By 1935 the figure had fallen to 12 cwt. The figures for landings per day's absence of individual fish tell the same story. Thus in 1906 a trawler's average landings of haddock for each day's absence from port was 7·8 cwt., but by 1935 this figure had fallen to 1·9 cwt. When fish become more difficult to catch, it seems reasonable to assume that there are fewer of them available.

These figures in themselves show quite convincingly that fish were more difficult to catch in the North Sea in 1935 than they were in 1906. Figures alone, however, do not always tell the whole story. In the thirty years under consideration the fishing power of the trawlers had been considerably increased. The average tonnage of the North Sea fleet in 1906 was 177 tons, whereas by 1935 it had risen to 257 tons. The importance of this increase in trawler size is that larger trawlers use bigger trawls and therefore have greater fishing power than smaller ones. In addition, the introduction of the Vigneron-Dahl modification to the standard otter trawl in the 1920's had increased its fishing power by at least 25 per cent. All this means that a 1906 trawler with its gear would have caught considerably less than 1·9 cwt. of haddock per day's absence had it fished on the North Sea grounds in 1935, and therefore that the stocks of fish on these grounds had in fact been more seriously depleted than the comparative figures indicate.

Britain is, of course, only one of many nations whose trawlers share in the North Sea harvest. Figures for total North Sea landings in all countries also throw interesting light on the overfishing problem. The total average yearly catch of haddock, the most important of all the fish in the North Sea, by all fishing vessels over the period 1910–18 was 121 million kilos. From 1922 to 1929 it was 128 kilos, but from 1930 to 1936 the average had fallen to 94 million kilos. During the period from 1910 until 1936 we know that fishing power was steadily increasing both through the increase in trawler size and through the introduction of the Vigneron-Dahl trawl modification. Hence in the 1930's we have a much larger total fishing power than in 1910, producing a substantially smaller yield of fish— a clear-cut indication of overfishing.

Further proof of overfishing on the North Sea grounds can be produced by comparing the state of affairs on these and other home fishing grounds with that in more distant waters. As the stocks on home grounds have become increasingly overfished, so the fishermen have tended to exploit fishing grounds farther away from port where stocks are more plentiful. In consequence the importance of the home fishing grounds has steadily decreased so that whereas in 1905 the North Sea provided 60 per cent of all the white fish landed at English ports, by 1937 it accounted for only 12 per cent. At the present time the more distant the grounds are from the European fishing ports, the more dense are their stocks of fish, and therefore the greater their yield for a given effort. This is shown very clearly by comparing the total landings per day's absence from Home, Middle and Distant grounds. In 1937 the figure for Home grounds—that is, the North Sea and other waters near to the English coast—was 12·5 cwt. per day's absence. From Middle grounds, comprising the waters of the northern part of the North Sea, of the Faeroe Islands, and of the west of Scotland and Ireland, it was 29·4 cwt. The distant grounds of Iceland, Bear Island and the Barentz Sea yielded 77·8 cwt. Convincing evidence though these figures may be that Home waters are heavily overfished compared with those farther away, they are nevertheless biased in that they do not take into account the fact that trawlers fishing the more distant grounds spend much more time travelling between the ports and the grounds, and therefore less time fishing, than do those which fish in Home waters. Yields expressed in weight of fish caught per hundred hours' actual fishing time would be more accurate, and would show an even greater discrepancy between the three groups.

Another sign of overfishing is an increase in the proportion of small fish in the total catch suggesting, as one would expect, that large numbers of fish are caught before they have reached maturity. Here again there are relevant figures to show that during the last fifty years large fully-grown fish have become progressively less common, especially in the North Sea. For market purposes haddock are graded into three sizes, large, medium and small. Between 1906 and 1914 haddock landed at English ports from the North Sea contained 50 per cent small, 30 per cent medium and 20 per cent large by weight. By 1937 the proportion of small fish was more than 90 per cent, and there were only 2 per cent of large fish. If the figures were quoted as numbers of fish instead of weight of fish, the reduction in large and medium fish which had taken place over this period would seem even more striking. North Sea plaice stocks have undergone a similar reduction in the average size of fish. In 1893 58 per cent of all plaice landed from the North Sea were over 13 inches long, a figure which by 1937 had fallen to 21 per cent.

Overfishing has thus produced a great change in size distribution of the various fish stocks in the North Sea. Since fish grow steadily until some years after they have reached maturity the size distribution in any stock will give a fairly good indication of the age distribution. This, however, can be independently determined by examining all the fish in sample hauls from the main grounds. So that no fish escape, the cod end of the trawl is covered with fine-mesh netting, which will retain the smaller fish that are normally not captured.

In the 1890's it was discovered that the age of carp could be ascertained by counting the rings on its scales. Subsequently the scale-reading technique was found to give reliable results for most of our food fishes. Later it was found that the age of a plaice could be estimated more reliably by examining a small bone in the ear of the fish, called the earstone or otolith. By these methods the scientists are able to determine the age distribution in sample hauls, and so to carry out extensive investigations on various fish populations. The age grouping of a lightly fished stock can be compared with that of an overfished stock, and a particular age group can be followed through from year to year, so that the extent to which its numbers become depleted can be ascertained.

In a stock very lightly fished it was found that the mature fish showed a great age range, a high proportion being many years past the age of first maturity, whereas in a heavily fished stock very few fish survived many years after reaching maturity, thus confirming conclusions arrived at by other methods. In 1929 very few haddocks survived beyond their eighth year in the heavily fished North Sea populations, whereas in the Rockall population, at that time only lightly fished, haddock up to fourteen years of age were quite common.

Mortality rates as worked out by following a particular year class and noting how its abundance decreased from year to year showed clearly that fishing could be the main cause of death in a well-fished stock. In some stocks the annual mortality rate due to fishing has been found to be as high as 70 per cent.

Results obtained by age analysis of sample hauls have been confirmed by large-scale marking experiments, which have been particularly successful with plaice. Large samples of a particular year class are marked, and the numbers caught and returned in each succeeding year are tabulated. During a large-scale investigation from 1929 to 1932 no fewer than 20,000 young plaice were marked in the southern North Sea. After the second year the numbers returned indicated a fishing rate equal to 73 per cent of the available stock. Small wonder therefore that few fish older than four or five years are found on these fishing grounds.

For some of the most important work on the overfishing problem we are indebted to Dr. C. G. J. Petersen, who was Director of the Danish Biological Station. He stated the whole problem in terms of food supply which, he said, was limited for any fish population. If most of the old fish were allowed to live until they died of old age, as in an unfished or lightly fished stock, then they would consume a proportion of this available food. Having already reached full size, however, they would not use it to make more fish flesh, but merely to maintain their weight. At the same time the food they consumed would not be available for immature fish, which would have used it for rapid growth—that is production of fish flesh. Thus, Petersen concluded, it is possible to have a state of underfishing where considerable numbers of old fish live on beyond the time when they have reached full size.

Petersen also showed that excessive numbers of fish of any age in relation to the available food supply were just as detrimental to the total growth rate of a fish stock as too many old fish. If there were too many young fish, they would be able to get little more food than they needed for maintaining life, and consequently their rate of growth would be slow.

The history of the plaice fishery in the Kattegat bears out Petersen's contentions. At the beginning of the century there was little fishing of this stock, which consequently consisted of a large number of slow-growing fish. As the intensity of fishing increased, more and more of the older fish were caught, leaving more food for the younger fish, which therefore grew more quickly. By 1920 the total population was much reduced, but because of the faster growth the total yield from the fishery was easily maintained.

The ideal for all fishing grounds would be so to regulate the rate of fishing that the balance between the numbers of surviving fish of all ages and the food supply was such as to give the maximum yearly production of fish flesh—that is, a fast-growing stock. With such a stock, not only would a high total yield be maintained, but also each trawler's catch per day's absence from port would be high, and the industry would flourish. Besides regulating the total catch, stocks can be benefited by fixing minimum mesh sizes for nets in an effort to prevent too many of the smaller immature fish from being caught.

Such an optimum fishing rate would have to be worked out for each fishing ground, by watching the stocks of both mature and immature fish and the rate of fishing over a number of years. Variations in brood years would have to be allowed for. As a particularly good year class approached maturity, the permitted catch could be increased for a year or two, while a poor class would necessitate a corresponding reduction in fishing.

## Controlled Exploitation—A Population Problem

Consideration of the information from the last sixty years relating to the North Sea fishing grounds leaves no doubt that an advanced state of overfishing has been reached. On Petersen's theory a permanent substantial reduction in the fishing power of these grounds would eventually result in a more efficient fishery giving perhaps a greater annual yield than at present. Certainly the present weight of fish taken from the grounds would be maintained with far less expenditure of fishing effort, and the proportion of large fish in the catches would be much greater. It seems desirable, therefore, that agreement should be reached among the European nations to reduce the total fishing power in the North Sea. These conclusions, however, are based on a theory (derived, it is true, from a great accumulation of facts), and fishermen are practical people. Schemes that seem ideal on paper do not always work out in practice—snags arise which were not foreseen, or it is realized too late that certain important factors have not been taken into account.

Fortunately, however, the suggested cure for overfishing is not based on theory alone, and we have concrete evidence that substantial reduction in the rate of fishing on an overfished ground does result in a maintenance, or even in an increase, in the total landings, and in a marked improvement in the size distribution of the catch. During the two world wars fishing was unavoidably reduced on all fishing grounds, allowing the depleted stocks of fish to recuperate, with the result that when full-scale fishing was resumed after the end of hostilities, the yield per day's absence was considerably above what it had been at the outbreak of war, and the catches contained a much higher proportion of larger fish. On both occasions, however, a high rate of fishing soon reduced the stocks once more to a state of overfishing, and the possibility of regulating the fisheries at an economic level passed away.

For those who doubt that regulation would work out in practice, there is convincing proof available in the story of the Pacific halibut fishery, which has been regulated at an economic level since 1932 by agreement between the United States and Canadian Governments. The history of this fishery shows all the stages in the growth of a fishery to the point of overfishing and beyond.

Off the west coast of North America there are numerous banks on which halibut flourish. Until about sixty years ago only small quantities were caught by the local inhabitants for their own needs. Then came the transcontinental railways, and with them the possibility of opening up inland markets. So a modern fishery grew up, and as the number of boats increased, so did the total catch. Until about 1910 the catch per boat remained high, and the fishery was still confined to the inshore waters along 500 miles or so of coast northward from Vancouver.

The limit of these banks had now been reached, and the catch per boat began to fall away, indicating the onset of overfishing. From 1906, when the landings per unit of gear on the original banks was 300 lb., there was a drop to 50 lb. per unit of gear by 1926, and 35 lb. by 1929. From 1910, in order to maintain the total catch, banks progressively farther away from port had to be visited, until the fishery extended along 2,000 miles of coast. Thus in order merely to maintain the total landings, more and more fishing effort had to be expended. As Dr. W. F. Thompson, to whom we are indebted for the details of this history, puts it: 'The result was a maintained total catch, hiding successive depletions of bank after bank, until the yield that came originally from 500 miles was stretched over 2,000 miles of coast from Oregon to Bering Sea.' And, one might add, this necessitated a corresponding increase in the size of the fleet and in the number of fishermen engaged.

Then in 1932 the United States and Canada agreed to fix the total amount of halibut that could be caught on the Pacific grounds at a figure substantially below the average for the 1920's. Very quickly the stocks began to recover, and with them the amount of fish landed per unit of gear. In a few years the fishermen were landing the permitted total in five months, as against the nine months it would have taken them previously.

Similar control on the North Sea grounds would be extremely difficult, because so many nations share the fishing there. However, something can be done by way of fixing a minimum size of mesh for trawls, which will reduce the adverse effect of trawling on the immature fish, and also by fixing size limits for each species below which it is illegal to land and sell them. This discourages trawlers from fishing on those grounds where immature fish congregate in the greatest numbers. Such regulations are in force, but they can never bring about a substantial improvement so long as the fishing power remains too great for the fish stocks.

A similar problem to that of overfishing has faced the whaling industry during the past few decades. The history of whaling goes back several centuries, when the slower species were hunted in the North Atlantic from open boats. The old whalers distinguished these slow whales as right whales, to distinguish them from the wrong whales, which were the swifter rorqual whales. These moved too fast to be caught and harpooned. During the seventeenth, eighteenth and nineteenth centuries the three species hunted were the Greenland and Biscay right whales in northern waters, and the sperm whales in many seas in all parts of the world.

Whales are of two kinds, the toothed whales, which feed on large prey, and the whalebone whales, which filter out from the sea water with their massive plates of whalebone or baleen small shrimp-like crustaceans. Only the sperm whale among the toothed whale has any economic importance, and is the only species to attain a size comparable to that of the larger whalebone whales, attaining a maximum length of seventy feet. The

## Controlled Exploitation—A Population Problem

Greenland and Biscay whales are both whalebone whales, and both were almost hunted to extinction in earlier times.

The Greenland or Arctic right whale grows to about sixty-five feet in length, and has an enormous head extending for about one third of the total body length, and containing as many as 400 separate baleen plates each about twelve feet long. It lives mainly in the seas around Greenland, where it swims along the margins of the ice-fields where there is a great abundance of the tiny crustaceans which form the bulk of their food. From the beginning of the seventeenth century these whales were ruthlessly hunted by British and Dutch whalers, until by the end of the nineteenth century they were practically extinct.

The southern right whale or Biscay whale suffered a similar fate much earlier. From the tenth century onwards it was hunted off the western coast of France by the Basque whalers. By the end of the sixteenth century it was becoming very rare, and was probably only saved from final extinction by the timely discovery in 1596 of the Greenland whale. The most valuable product of the whaling industry is the oil which is extracted from the thick layer of blubber beneath the skin of the whale. The purpose of this layer is to insulate the body of the creature and thus to cut down the loss of heat from a warm-blooded mammal living in cold water. Other important by-products are meat meal, bone meal, liver oil, liver meal and frozen whale meat. Every part of the whale that is of any value is used. In earlier times the spermaceti contained in an enormous cavity in the head of the sperm whale was of considerable value, but to-day has little worth. At the body temperature of the whale it is a liquid, but as it cools it sets to a soft wax-like substance, which at one time was used as an important ingredient of the best wax candles.

As the whales of the North Atlantic became scarce towards the end of the nineteenth century, the whalers turned their attention to the fast rorqual whales of the Antarctic. Modern whaling had been made possible by the invention in 1860, by a Norwegian whaling captain Svend Foyn, of the harpoon gun. This, mounted in the bows of a fast ship, made it possible to pursue and capture the fast whales which were too swift to be caught with hand harpoons in open boats. Traditional hand harpooning of sperm whales, with all its excitement and danger, is still practised in the Azores.

Modern Antarctic whaling began with the establishment of the first whaling station in South Georgia in 1904. In that year only one catcher operated, and took 195 whales which yielded 5,302 barrels of whale oil. Thereafter the industry grew, and gradually other stations were opened both in South Georgia and elsewhere. Later the shore station was gradually replaced by the large factory ship, on which the blubber was removed from the whales, and all the other useful parts of the animal processed. Attached to each factory ship are about a dozen fast catchers. The largest factory ships are vessels of about 15,000 tons carrying as many as 500 men who are able to cut up and sort a sixty-ton whale in an hour. The pieces are sent to various parts of the ship, where the oil is extracted from the blubber and the various by-products are prepared. The oil is then stored in special tanks and the by-products in appropriate compartments, the whale meat being kept in huge cold stores.

Antarctic whaling is concerned in the main with four species of rorqual whales, the blue whale, the fin whale, the humpback whale and the sei whale, and the season is based upon their natural habits. During the Antarctic summer they roam along the edge of the pack ice feeding upon the vast shoals of krill which flourish there at this time of the year. It is then that they are able to lay down vast stores of fat in the form of blubber, and it is after a few months of this feeding that they yield the greatest quantity of oil. At the end of the summer many, if not most of them, travel northwards to warmer sub-tropical waters.

Here, although they will lose less heat, they do not feed, for the krill only exist in the cold Antarctic waters, and they seem incapable of feeding on any other kind of animal life. So they gradually use up their fat stores, and thus return in the spring with a much thinner layer of blubber. The cow whales give birth to their young when they are in the warmer waters, so that during their time of fasting they have to feed their calves as well as keep themselves going.

As the number of whalers steadily increased it was realized by the principal whaling countries that some kind of regulation might be eventually necessary to prevent the stocks from becoming permanently depleted. As early as 1924 the British Colonial Office set up a committee to investigate the habits of the Antarctic whales so that the necessary information might be available should it become necessary to regulate the catching. By the middle 1930's it became obvious that the Antarctic rorqual whales were heading for extinction if catching continued to increase at the current rate, and in 1937 the principal whaling countries signed a convention agreeing to a number of conditions to govern whaling in the Antarctic. Among the provisions of the Convention was an agreement to limit the season to three months. Minimum lengths for each species, below which it was illegal to catch them, were also fixed.

During the war the whales enjoyed a respite, but after it was all over they were hunted with renewed vigour and improved technique and fishing power. Those interested, however, acted quickly, and the International Convention for the Regulation of Whaling was signed in 1946. The Convention recognized the imminent dangers of over-exploitation, and the need for conservation by regulating the number of whales caught. The Whaling Commission, an international body set up to operate the Convention, meets once a year to draw up the regulations for the ensuing season. Its particular function is to fix the total number of whales which may be caught. This number depends upon the species, since the different species vary considerably in size.

The annual permissible take is reckoned in blue whale units, each of which is one blue whale, two fin whales, two and a half humpback whales or six sei whales. In recent years the limit has been fixed at a figure of about 16,000 blue whale units. The actual catching is controlled from the Bureau of International Whaling Stastistics at Sandefjord in Norway. The season begins during the first few days of January, and thereafter each whaling factory radios its catch to the Bureau weekly. When the total catch begins to approach the limit for the season these messages are sent in daily, and as soon as the figure is reached messages are sent out to the whole whaling fleet declaring the season closed. This regulation of whaling is one of the finest examples of international co-operation in the interests of conserving economically valuable animals, and could well serve as a model for similar international regulation of the exploitation of other economically valuable animal populations. Fears have been expressed in recent years that the annual permissible limits are being set too high, and that the average age of the whales caught is gradually falling, thus indicating a gradual state of overfishing. If this proves to be true it seems likely that the International Convention will be able to correct this trend by fixing lower permissible limits for a few years while the stocks recover.

# 3

## Conservation in National Parks
## and Nature Reserves

★

The first realization that some form of nature reserve or national park was the only solution to the problem of the steady but alarming general decrease in the wildlife of the world through the activities of man took place in America about ninety years ago, when the world's first national park, the famous Yellowstone, was established by the U.S. Government in 1872 'as a pleasure ground for the benefit and enjoyment of the people'. This park, extending for more than two million acres, was not so much concerned with the preservation of the American fauna as its natural landscape and everything which went with it.

The first active steps to preserve the animal life of a country by the creation of a nature reserve specifically for this purpose was due to President Kruger, and it was a continuation of his initial efforts which led to the creation of the most famous and perhaps the most important of all the world's national parks, the Kruger. Because of its importance as the pioneer animal park the story of its origin and development is of particular interest. As early as 1884 Kruger drew attention to the fact that the game animals of the Transvaal were diminishing at an alarming rate, and proposed to the Volksraad, the Transvaal parliament, the advisability of setting aside a sanctuary where animals might find refuge protected from persecution. He found, however, little support for his ideas.

Four years later, however, he submitted a further resolution urging 'the desirability of the Volksraad authorizing the Government in view of the rapid extermination of game in the South African Republic to prohibit totally the hunting of game on some portions of Government land and to draw up the necessary regulations and penalties relative thereto'. In a speech supporting the motion he suggested two possible areas as being suitable for consideration. The resolution was passed, but nothing further happened for several years, until on 6th September 1895 a group of members submitted the following historical motion: 'The undersigned, seeing that nearly all big game in the Republic have been exterminated, and that those animals still remaining are becoming less day by day, so that there is a danger of their becoming altogether extinct in the near future, request to be permitted to depart from the order paper to discuss the desirability of authorizing the Government to proclaim as a Government Game Reserve, where killing of game shall altogether be prohibited, certain portions of the district of Lydenburg, being Government land, where most of the big game species are still to be found, to wit, the territory situated between the Crocodile and the Sabi Rivers with boundaries as follows....' The boundaries which were then suggested were finally adopted as those of the Sabi Game Reserve when it was set up in 1898. On 26th March in that year President Kruger himself issued the proclamation which established the reserve. Merely to proclaim a reserve, however, is not to bring it into being. To translate a proclamation into a reality a great deal of hard work is necessary, and a great deal of determined opposition from vested interests has to be overcome.

The story of the next quarter of a century, during which all kinds of problems had to be tackled and opponents won over or defeated, is of great importance to the history of the national park movement, because it is to a large extent the story of every other reserve and park which has been created and developed during the past sixty years.

Right from the start there were difficulties. Within eighteen months of the proclamation the South African war broke out, and in the intervening period it had been possible to do little more than draw up the precise boundaries and fix penalties for shooting and poaching game within them. For the duration of the war it was impossible to put into effect any conservation programme, and the poachers had a free hand. In addition Steinacker's Horse were stationed in the reserve, and much of their meat supplies had to come from local game population. Fortunately, however, the adjutant was a convert to the idea of game preservation, and towards the end of the war his soldiers did much valuable work in curbing the activities of poachers.

When the war was over the responsibility for the future development of the Sabi Reserve passed to the British administration. Fortunately several factors were in favour of the reserve being given the support it so badly needed. Just prior to the war Abel Chapman, a distinguished British naturalist, had toured the district, and had been very impressed with its future possibilities as a game reserve. Subsequently he drew up a comprehensive draft for such a reserve. Largely as a result of this draft the Sabi Reserve was re-proclaimed by the British authorities as soon as hostilities ceased. Sir Godfrey Lagden, who was appointed Commissioner for Native Affairs in the Transvaal, was very interested in wildlife preservation, and assumed personal responsibility for the reserve. Early in 1902 he met the late Lt.-Col. J. Stevenson-Hamilton, who had spent some time exploring the big game hunting in what is now Northern Rhodesia, and who was also very keen on the idea of fauna conservation. As a result he was invited to take charge of the new reserve for the time being. This was a fortunate meeting and a fortunate appointment, because for the next forty-four

53

years he was destined to guide the development of the Sabi Game Reserve until it had become well established as the famous Kruger National Park, the greatest of all the national parks, and the model which was to be followed by the many similar parks which were destined to be created during the twentieth century. He himself was to become one of the greatest names associated with modern fauna preservation. In a fascinating book *South African Eden* he has left a vivid account of the struggles and disappointments which he had to face before the Kruger Park was finally established beyond the possibilities of challenge.

His appointment dated from 1st July 1902, and shortly afterwards, he tells us, 'I was recommended to go to Lydenburg, and, arrived there, was fitted out with some government transport. Thence, with no very clear idea of what was I was expected to do, except, as Sir Godfrey had instructed, to make myself "generally disagreeable", I started out on the Great Adventure.' Any illusions he might have had that his task would be an easy one involving routine administration were soon shattered. The majority of the animals had been so disturbed by shooting that they had migrated to other areas, and it was to take years of patient endeavour to lure them back again. The accommodation available for him and his staff was of the most primitive kind, and the activities of the poachers were a major and urgent problem.

Having surveyed the reserve, Stevenson-Hamilton decided to make his headquarters for the time being at Crocodile Bridge. Here there was an almost derelict iron shack, but without the materials for building this would have to do. 'The flies therein were equalled only by the rats,' he wrote, 'with which the place positively swarmed, consequent no doubt on its formerly having been used as a mealie store. At night they steeplechased about between the ceiling and the roof, making a terrific din, as they scampered over the corrugated iron, sometimes seeming to fall down in heaps between it and the panelling, and then scrambling up again, scratching, squeaking, and rushing about without cessation. Eventually I got a cat, and put her up in the roof, but the rats must have proved too much for her, as she deserted.'

Lack of suitable accommodation, however, was merely an irritating inconvenience, but the native poachers were a major problem. Stevenson-Hamilton found himself up against not a few individuals, but a whole tribe. 'The M'Hlangane tribe, who regarded the Game Reserve as their special preserve, were, from natural aptitude and long usage, man and boy of them, in one way or another, hunting experts, and what they did not know about the various methods of compassing the destruction of wild animals was not worth knowing. Snares of every conceivable pattern, and dogs, were the methods employed. Some of the former were designed for, and were capable of hoisting an animal of the size of a buffalo by one leg, there to hang suspended for an indefinite period until someone visited the trap; others caught the foot in a cunningly devised ring of sticks, to which a heavy log was attached. For small animals falling log traps were in favour, but iron gins were also used whenever obtainable. Dogs bailed up the larger antelopes, not a difficult matter, since most of them, especially waterbuck, when pursued, usually sought a pool of water, there to stand at bay, and of course were easily despatched in this situation by assagais. Warthog were chased to ground in ant-bear or porcupine holes, where the dogs held them earthed until their masters arrived to dig them out.'

In the early stages everything seemed to go in favour of the Sabi Reserve. By early in 1904 the original 1,800 square miles had been increased to about 12,000 square miles by the temporary addition of a great deal of private farmland. The owners of these farms had willingly given the authority for the reserve staff to protect the game on their lands for an initial period of five years, the aim being to increase the total game both in the original reserve and in the surrounding districts from which the reserve might hope to replenish its own diminished supplies.

The whole idea of fauna preservation was, however, not without its vigorous opponents, and there was always the fear that the authority of the reserve might be removed overnight. After all it had been established by a proclamation, and could just as easily be destroyed by the same means. It had little actual legal status. There was a considerable body of influential opinion which was against fauna preservation as an ideal. In the view of these people the expenditure of public money on game preservation was unjustified, except for a certain measure of conservation to provide an increased stock of game for future shooting.

At this time Stevenson-Hamilton himself had no very clear idea of what the future held, or what he was really aiming for. After returning from a visit to London in 1905 he wrote: 'What then exactly was I working for, beyond the mere enjoyment of the life itself, and the interest inseparable from all development? While in London, I had been a good deal in touch with wild life preservation matters, which were then beginning to arouse interest in certain circles, mainly through the efforts of Mr. E. N. Buxton, who had shortly before founded the Society for the Preservation of the Fauna of the Empire. I had incidentally heard a good deal about the American national parks, and of their success as a public attraction. Would it conceivably be possible to wean the South African public from its present attitude towards the wild animals of its own country, which was that of regarding them either as a convenient source of exploitation, or as an incubus hindering the progress of civilization? It seemed pretty hopeless. The low-veld was wild, dangerous, unhealthy; there were not many scenic attractions; few people had any interest in wild animals unless they were dead. There were no roads either in or leading to the reserves, and fortunately so, since they would only have provided easy access for shooting parties. There was no money for development, nor likely to be; in fact at the commencement of each financial year I gave a sigh of relief when I found our small grant of £5,000 still on the estimates, a sum which barely sufficed to pay salaries and wages, with nothing over to construct dwellings for the staff, or to carry out the hundred and one improvements I had in mind. Government in fact, beyond paying the monthly wage bill, left us in the main to shift for ourselves. But for the debris of the abandoned railway, and the various remains of old buildings scattered about, the former owners of which had disappeared, we should have been very hard put to it. The former provided picks, shovels, axes and wheelbarrows, besides quantities of nondescript scrap metal, the latter mainly more or less serviceable sheets of corrugated iron. Yet Government was more sympathetic, on the whole, than the public.

'Obviously one could just carry on and hope; but at least I had now a definite goal to work for, which was much to the good. I sent for and read all the literature available concerning the American national parks, especially the Yellowstone, and was astonished at the vast amount of money which the U.S. Government thought it worth while to spend on it, and at the public enthusiasm displayed. The American public must surely be very different from ours! The main object at present must be to use every effort to increase our depleted fauna, hoping that some day it might be recognized as a definite asset; as something more admirable alive than dead. Long years—more than twenty in fact—were to pass before the goal then visualized was attained; and many set backs, disappointments, and dangers to the Reserves were to intervene; but the then incredible thing did actually come to pass, and I shall always think of that day in Hannemann's Hotel as a red letter one, on which first faintly dawned the Idea which later found its culmination in the creation of the Kruger National Park, and of Hannemann himself as *deus ex machina*.'

For the next nine years until the outbreak of war the reserve survived, but its future still remained in doubt. Sometimes it seemed that support for the idea of fauna preservation was growing, but at other times it seemed that the days of the reserve were numbered. With the coming of union in 1910 it seemed to Stevenson-Hamilton that the prospects of establishing the reserve eventually as a national park were more bright, but within a few years he was doomed to further disappointment. In 1912 the agreements with the local farmers, which had been extended after the end of the original five years, finally came to an end. It was then that the Government gave way to the pressure exerted on it and agreed to allow winter grazing in the reserve, and this, Stevenson-Hamilton realized, would have an extremely detrimental effect on the game in the reserve.

From now on the public agitation against the reserve and all that it stood for increased steadily. Finally, in response to pressure, the Government agreed to appoint a commission to inquire into the whole question of whether there was any justification for continuing its existence. Right through 1917 and 1918 the commission sat periodically, and the supporters of the reserve became more and more despondent as the time drew near for the publication of its report. Contrary to expectation, however, the commissioners had during the course of their visits to the reserve became converted to the idea of fauna preservation. Not only did they report in favour of its continuance, but even suggested that it should in the future be transformed into a national park for the enjoyment of the public.

One paragraph is worth quoting in this connection: 'In the course of our investigations we were not a little struck by the uselessness of having these magnificent Reserves merely for the preservation of the fauna—in an area practically unknown and, by the effect of a somewhat stringent policy, made to a great extent inaccessible to the bulk of the people—a policy which it will be increasingly difficult to maintain as applied to so large an area . . . for these and other reasons we recommend that the policy of the Administration should be directed toward the creation of the area ultimately as a great national park where the natural and prehistoric conditions of our country can be preserved for all time.' Some years were to elapse, however, and many set backs endured, before the policy recommended by the commission was finally adopted.

In 1921 and 1922 the end of the reserve seemed in sight. The opposition seemed to be steadily increasing in power, while at the same time the Government interest in the idea seemed to diminish, presumably under the influence of what it thought was hostile public opinion. The farmer wanted to take over the reserve for grazing, the industrialist wanted it for prospecting, and the hunter for game shooting. This, however, represented the lowest ebb of the reserve's fortunes.

An apparently insignificant event which took place in 1923 had an unexpected effect on public opinion. The South African Railways began a fortnightly tourist service during the winter months to points of interest in the Transvaal, and included the Sabi Game Reserve in its itinerary. This part of the tour rapidly became the highlight, and the reactions of the travellers to the reserve were most encouraging. 'The interest betrayed by the public in the animals,' wrote Stevenson-Hamilton, 'and the remarks I overheard when mixing with the passengers, made me at last confident that, could only our national park scheme mature, it would become popular, and therefore an asset to the country, and it was beyond measure encouraging to feel that the South African public, despite tradition, might be content to look at animals without wanting to kill them.

'Directly the South African Railway Administration realized that the Sabi Reserve held potential publicity value, it at once became, in the person of Mr. Hoye, the general manager, a wholehearted supporter of its development into a national park.'

From now on the opposition gradually weakened and support

for the proposed national park grew. After much preliminary negotiation the Sabi Game Reserve became the Kruger National Park with the passing of the National Parks Act on 31st May 1926. From then onwards development continued steadily, until a tour of the Kruger Park became one of the most spectacular journeys it was possible for the public to make in any part of the world.

The success of the Kruger Park after so many years of struggle and determined opposition was much more than a fortunate conclusion to the struggle to preserve the wildlife of the Transvaal. It was the stimulus for the foundation of nature reserves and national parks all over the world. Without the example of the Sabi Game Reserve it is unlikely that the national park movement would have achieved the results that it has done. It would be wrong, however, to assume that all parks are now safe from opposition. Vested interests have still to be reckoned with, and only constant vigilance and vigorous defence of the ideal will prevent further encroachment on the dwindling stocks of wild life in all parts of the world. The ultimate value of the national park and the reserve is that, unlike the other methods of preservation with which this book is mainly concerned, they aim to preserve whole populations of animals and not merely individual species which have become rare.

To give an account of all the national parks and reserves of the world would be quite impossible here. A whole book would be necessary to do the subject justice. It is more important to underline the importance of the parks and reserves, and indeed of fauna preservation itself. One of the most eloquent pleas for conservation in modern times was made by Mervyn Cowie, Director of the Royal National Parks of Kenya, in an address which he gave to the Fauna Preservation Society in 1955. Although he deals with Africa, where the problem of conservation is more acute than it is in any other part of the world, what he has to say is applicable to every part of the world. I can think of no better way of concluding this chapter than by quoting extensively from this most important survey of the problem as it exists today.

'Why do we try to preserve wild animals? Why do we set aside delightful scenes of nature? Why do we establish open spaces and national parks? Would it not be better to accept here and now that man in his dominion over all the lesser creatures has every right to divest the land of animals, trees, or anything else which may stand in his way, or hinder him in exploiting the earth for the alleged well-being of mankind? Vast sums are spent in the larger continents to control domestic animal diseases; greater sums are spent in denuding the face of the earth of its natural cover, so that there can be more room for cattle, crops, factories and cities, in an attempt to meet the insatiable clamour of millions of human beings. Should we not pause to assess what irreplaceable assets are being endangered by this scramble and to what extent those assets contribute to men's peace of mind?

'Africa is the last stronghold of wild nature and today is surging under the various forces of human achievement. It is a harsh country which retaliates, often by means quite unpredicted, wherever man seeks to interfere with the forces of nature. Droughts, locust invasions, plagues and political upheavals, all militate against the enterprises of man in Africa. What will he achieve and at what cost if he succeeds in his endeavours and converts the greater part of this dark continent into a highly civilized economy? However much the great machines of modern invention tear through the soil, Africa, left to itself, reverts in a remarkably short time to its original state; but never can wild animals, once destroyed, be recreated. The balance between man and beast, between beast and vegetation, between life and death, has been maintained through the centuries, and by a force for which even in this atomic age nothing can be substituted—neither can this force be defied.

## Conservation in National Parks and Nature Reserves

'Let us accept then that only in certain parts of Africa can man now go forward with his destructive plans and harness the potential of this great continent for his immediate requirements. Even where he does, let him assess whether he is making Africa, and the world, a better place, where man is happier or more peaceful. Only future generations will be truly qualified to make this assessment, for they will find that many of those things which once inspired peaceful enjoyment, and the scenes in wild nature which captured the imagination, have ceased to exist. The case for preservation is therefore intangible. We who have the responsibility of administering certain territories in Africa, must recognize that in them we have the world's greatest abundance of wild animal life. It is not ours to dispose of as we please; we hold it in trust.

'The Fauna Preservation Society stands in the position today of being an association founded on British tradition, uniting men of fair will, who are prepared to champion the cause of the lesser creatures. At no time in its history has it faced a bigger challenge than is held out to it today in Africa.

'It would be illogical to seek the protection of all wild life, since there must be development. There will surely also be increases in population, and there must be food for millions of human mouths. It is, however, reasonable that, before it is too late, Africa should be divided into zones; so that each claimant for the use of the land can have a fair share. In this division there must be a place for the wild animal. Stock farmers cannot range their cattle with lions, nor can the wheat farmer allow his crops to be plundered by thousands of grass-eating antelopes. And so, on the one hand there must be areas for human development and on the other hand let me plead for areas for total protection of nature.

'It is farcical to think that a line on a map described as a national park will ensure the survival of all the species of game within it, unless that area is faunally and ecologically complete and is properly administered. It is equally farcical to think that man and his cattle can share an area with game, for when Africa in its harshness revolts, when waterholes dry up and grass becomes scarce, then man and his cattle take what is left, and the beasts of the field perish. Thousands of square miles of British Africa, which in living memory carried millions of head of game, are now almost bare. In some countries hundreds of thousands of wild animals have been deliberately shot to make room for more cattle. Unless this destruction is checked, and unless it is made possible for the wild creatures to breed, nature's great balance in Africa will be upset and the remnants of its wild life will vanish.

'A gloomy picture, indeed, but judge the future on the trend of the past and the conclusion is inescapable. National parks, game reserves, protected areas and other little pockets enshrined for the safety of wild animals, give no more than lip service to the cause of preservation, unless they are adequate, wisely chosen, properly administered and ecologically complete. The challenge to the Fauna Preservation Society, at least within the territories in Africa administered by Great Britain, is to strive for this cause with resolve and determination. Every means should be used to convince a greedy and blinded world that there must be a change of heart if the wild animals are to be preserved.

'We must set aside suitable areas for total protection in which human claims are only secondary. We must ensure that the places already allocated to wild animals qualify in all respects as animal sanctuaries, and not merely as eventual cemeteries. Such places must remain inviolate and free of continual counter-claims. Budgets of colonial territories must contain a regular minimum share of finance for proper maintenance and development of established sanctuaries, and not be merely a subvention in times of plenty. The Judiciary must be convinced that the disastrous destruction of God's great beasts by ruthless poachers

*Conservation in National Parks and Nature Reserves*
is a crime against the rights of posterity, deserving really effective punishment. Colonial treasuries must be made to admit the monetary value of game in developing the vast potential of tourism. We must preserve properly if we mean to preserve at all, and we must do it now before it is too late.'

# 4

## Preservation in Captivity

*

Already several rare species owe their existence today to captivity, and as civilization advances more and more species are likely to disappear as wild animals, to be saved from final extinction only by the maintenance of captive breeding stocks. Behind the successful maintenance of breeding stocks of wild animals in captivity lies more than one hundred years of steady increase in our knowledge of the needs of captive animals. This progress has been of vital importance to the future of fauna preservation, and in this chapter we shall trace the gradual development of ways of maintaining wild animals successfully in captivity.

The Zoological Society of London was founded in 1826, and two years later opened its Regent's Park menagerie to the public for the first time. This was the first modern zoo, and its initial success inspired the foundation of other zoos both in Britain and in continental Europe. Although these early zoos had their successes, with few exceptions the animals exhibited did not survive for very long, and the breeding records were very disappointing.

The story of the development of modern methods of keeping wild animals in captivity so that they live through to old age and breed regularly really begins in an obscure fishmonger's shop in Hamburg in northern Germany in 1848. This shop was kept by Gottfried Hagenbeck who, in order to be independent of the local fish market, employed a number of fishermen and their boats under contract to deliver their entire catches to his shop. One day in March 1848 they caught six seals in their nets, and although it seemed unlikely that Hagenbeck could find any use for them, they respected their contract terms and duly delivered them to him. One would think that seals, with their ravenous appetites for fish, would be among the last creatures a fisherman would want on his premises, but Hagenbeck was always interested in animals, and thought that his customers might like to see the seals. So he decided to keep them in a back room behind the shop for a few days before sending them back to the sea, charging a penny to anyone who wanted to see them.

The response was terrific. All Hamburg, it seemed, was anxious to see a live seal at close quarters. This gave Hagenbeck an idea. If people who lived by the sea were so enthusiastic, how much more so might be people living in an inland town. So the seals were not returned to the sea. Instead, he took them to Berlin, where they were an even greater success. But the fish business had to be looked after, so Hagenbeck sold his seals and returned to Hamburg with a handsome profit from his first venture as animal exhibitor and salesman. From this small chance episode was destined to grow the largest and most famous animal business the world has ever seen. Encouraged by his initial success, Gottfried Hagenbeck soon opened a small public menagerie in Hamburg, and also became a dealer in animals. Both businesses flourished in a small way, but it was his son Carl who was to make the name of Hagenbeck famous throughout the world.

In 1859, at the age of fifteen, he took over control of the animal dealing side of the business. By this time the Hagenbecks had established contacts in many parts of the world, and were regularly importing almost every kind of animal for resale to zoos and travelling menageries. Under Carl Hagenbeck the business expanded rapidly, until by 1870 almost every wild animal caught in Africa and Asia passed through his hands. He was now employing his own men to catch the animals, and the sight of huge collections being loaded on board ship for despatch to Europe became a familiar one in half the ports of the world. It was soon Hagenbeck's proud boast that no matter what order he received, he and his collectors could fulfil it.

Important though these collecting activities were, it was in other fields that Carl Hagenbeck made his most important contributions to progress, revolutionizing both the methods of keeping wild animals in captivity and the methods of training performing animals for circus work. In these two fields he made a greater contribution than anyone else before or since his time.

Throughout the nineteenth century it was a well-established belief in all zoos that animals from tropical countries could only survive in temperate climates provided they were kept in houses heated to tropical temperatures. Too often this meant houses that were almost hermetically sealed, avoidance of draughts being almost a fetish. It was Hagenbeck who showed that mammals and birds from any part of the world could be acclimatized to northern European temperatures and remain perfectly healthy, even during the severest winter weather, when given free access to the open air. Under these conditions, too, they lived much longer than they did under the stuffy conditions which prevailed in zoos at that time. In his book *Beasts and Men*, published in 1909, Carl Hagenbeck describes how the idea of acclimatization originated.

'No fallacy is more widespread', he wrote, 'than that wild animals have to be kept throughout the winter carefully guarded from the effects of low temperatures. In Stellingen we keep lions, tigers, giraffes, ostriches and other tropical animals wandering freely about in the open, though they always have access to cover if they should wish for it. The first thing that put this idea into my head was seeing a chimpanzee in England in a cold winter in the sixties disporting himself in the snow on the roof of a large tent. When he became cold he went in and took up a position by the stove. Later on I came across a menagerie in Westphalia where the monkeys were also allowed out of doors in the winter. Here there was an arrangement for connecting the outer enclosure with the inner cages by flaps, so that the creatures could pass at will from one to the other. The inner cages were kept at a temperature of 55° to 65° F., but the monkeys used to come out even when the thermometer was below zero.

'It thus came about that very early in my career I pondered the question as to how far it was advisable to expose to our winter climate animals which came from tropical countries. The conclusion at which I arrived was attained by careful observation of the animals in my possession. My first experiment on the subject, however, was due to an accident rather than to any set purpose, and this occurred soon after I had been established at Neuer Pferdemarkt (1874). I received one day in September a very beautiful Indian Cyrus crane. This we placed in an open enclosure where it remained until nearly the beginning of winter. About that time I was, as so often happens to me, called away unexpectedly and did not get back till about a week later. During this week cold weather suddenly set in.

'I arrived back very late at night, but was awakened early next morning by the characteristic cry of my crane, which I had forgotten all about and which I had intended to transfer to a warm building. I hastened out to find the hoar frost lying on the ground, and expecting to see the crane frozen through with the cold. But to my astonishment I found him in the most boisterous health; and when I came up, expecting to see him on the point of death, he came dancing and fluttering round to greet me, filling the air with his loud cries. Seeing that he did not appear to have suffered in any way from the cold, I arranged in one corner of the enclosure a sort of recess with plenty of straw where he could obtain shelter from the cold. But never once during the snowstorms, wind, and rain of that long winter did he make any use of this recess. He maintained his health in as perfect condition as though he were in his own tropical climate. I date from this occurrence the inauguration of my settled custom of giving wild animals access to the open air to the greatest possible extent. From this time commenced those experiments on acclimatization which, since the founding of my animal park at Stellingen, have occupied a very large share of my attention.'

Stellingen, the world's first outdoor zoological gardens, was opened in 1897 on the outskirts of Hamburg, and even today, more than sixty years later, it still remains one of the most famous of all the world's zoos. Besides his experiments in acclimatization, Hagenbeck also experimented with novel ways of exhibiting animals to the best advantage, building artificial hills and valleys, and separating the animals from the public not by bars or railings, but with ditches too wide and deep for them to cross. In this way much of the appearance of captivity was removed.

It was fortunate to the further development of our knowledge of the keeping of wild animals in captivity that in 1903 Dr. Peter Chalmers Mitchell was appointed secretary to the Zoological Society of London. He came to the zoo already convinced of the value of fresh air. He knew of Hagenbeck's work, and was also very friendly with Dr. Leonard Hill, one of the pioneers of human hygiene, who had demonstrated the value of fresh air for human beings. Mitchell, however, had a hard struggle ahead of him, for nothing is more difficult than to convince men that new methods are superior to those they have used for half a lifetime.

Mitchell's first move was to examine the records of all deaths occurring at the zoo between the years 1870 and 1902 and compare the length of life of each type of animal in captivity with its expectation of life in the wild state, so far as this was known.

The results were convincing; it was quite clear that under existing methods an animal's expectation of life once it arrived at Regent's Park was very poor. Indeed, it so happened that the exceptional animals that had lived to a good age had almost always been those which had been provided with little or no artificial heat, and had had free access to the open air.

These statistics and conclusions were published in the *Proceedings of the Zoological Society*, Mitchell summing up as follows: 'The most fatal type of housing for any mammal or bird is confinement in the interior of a warmed house without free access to the open air. The conditions are very complex and I do not suggest that the provision of heat is in itself an evil. The ideal throughout the period of which my statistics were based, and which still maintains an evil existence in the minds of a majority of those who have to do with living animals, is that in the first place they have to be kept warm. Warmth having been secured, the more advanced persons have consented to, or even urged, the advantage of ventilation, moistening of the air, and so forth. The idea, however, is wrong. The first requisite is free access to the open air, the rest is light, space and cleanliness; these things having been secured, any form of heating that may be thought advisable may be added, in so far as it does not in any way interfere with the primary considerations.'

The almost universal conviction that heat above all was necessary for captive wild animals coming from tropical countries was based principally on two fallacies. First was the failure to realize that climate plays a comparatively minor part in determining the distribution of animals. Many kinds which are today restricted to tropical climates had a much wider distribution in earlier times, extending in many cases into temperate and even cold latitudes. The restrictions have occurred through a variety of causes not generally related to climate or temperature. The second fallacy was the uncritical assumption that all tropical animals lived all the time in sweltering heat. The facts are, of course, that cool periods can occur even during the daytime, while at night in many parts of the tropics it can be intensely cold. Furthermore, very few animals are happy in blazing tropical sunshine, most of them adopting some means of keeping cool, as for example by lying in water or mud, or hiding away under cover of dense forest.

Hence it is not really surprising that most tropical mammals and birds have proved able to acclimatize themselves quite readily to living out of doors in a temperate climate. Eventually, by sheer persistence, Mitchell succeeded in convincing the keepers. More and more animals were provided with outdoor cages, and indoor ventilation was introduced. The effect was marked. Almost every species showed a considerable increase in its length of life in captivity, and the general standard of health among the animals improved.

To Chalmers Mitchell, however, this was only a beginning, for it was to him that we owe the idea and achievement of Whipsnade, the world's first large-scale zoological park. Already in 1903, within a few months of his appointment as secretary, he had put forward a suggestion for establishing a country station where animals from Regent's Park could be sent for periods of rest and recuperation after illness. At this time, as well as on several future occasions when Mitchell raised the subject again, the society was not prepared to consider it. At last, however, he was able to convince the council of the society of the value of his proposal, and work started in 1928 on the conversion of a 500-acre farm to a zoological park. This work took three years to complete, and Whipsnade Park was opened to the public on 23rd May 1931.

In the intervening years since he first conceived the idea in 1903 Chalmers Mitchell was able to formulate the aims of a zoological park in greater detail. The principal aim was to present groups of animals living in natural surroundings and with a natural background of trees and sky. It was hoped that by

71

giving them sufficient space they would establish themselves as natural groups or herds, maintaining themselves by breeding, and exhibiting normal social behaviour such as would be impossible in the confined spaces available in zoological gardens. If these hopes were realized, then Whipsnade could play a leading part in the preservation of wild animals threatened with extinction, by maintaining small breeding groups.

From the point of view of fauna preservation the most important achievements at Whipsnade have been its phenomenal breeding successes. During the past two or three decades there have been notable improvements in the breeding of animals in captivity throughout the world. There are many reasons for this. Every zoo has, of course, been conducting experiments and increasing its own knowledge. Through publication of the results of these experiments in scientific journals and through increased facilities for travel, there has been a great improvement in the exchange of information between zoos. The ease of travel has also made it possible for zoo directors to pay frequent visits to other zoos for the purpose of discussion and exchange of information.

Many animals can be satisfactorily maintained in captivity, remaining healthy and apparently happy until they die of old age, having lived probably considerably longer than they would have done facing all the hazards of life in the wild state, yet they fail to breed. It is now appreciated that for many wild animals, if not all, the requirements for successful breeding are far more critical than those for mere healthy survival. Much of the recent work in zoos throughout the world has been concentrated on discovering these optimum conditions for as many species as possible, and in this work Whipsnade is playing a major part. One of the difficulties has been that optimum conditions for one species may be far from satisfactory for another species even though the two may be quite closely related. The common pool of knowledge today, though, is so big that it is reasonable to hope that the problems of keeping any animal in captivity and maintaining a breeding stock of almost any species could be solved in sufficient time if the animal became threatened with extinction.

It would of course be impossible to deal with all that has been learnt about the breeding of wild animals in captivity in a single chapter. We can, however, look at some of the outstanding examples to see what kind of information has been accumulated. The problem posed by bears was a particularly interesting one, because in fact they did breed quite often. The trouble was that their offspring never survived. The clue which finally led to the successful rearing of bears in captivity was an appreciation of the significance of the very unusual natural conditions under which bear cubs are reared in the wild state.

When the Whipsnade bear pit was constructed a number of underground dens were dug. The main purpose of these was to provide the bears with some shelter against bad weather. However, within a year of the pit being occupied for the first time, cubs were produced and successfully reared by the mother. Relying on her natural instinct she had hidden herself away in one of the shelters before her cubs were born and had stayed there for a couple of months. For the first few weeks at least she seemed to require little or no food. When she finally brought the cubs out for the first time they were already strong and well grown. It seemed then that although hibernation could normally be dispensed with, partial hibernation of the pregnant females was essential for the successful rearing of the cubs. What was needed, therefore, was a den to which the mothers could retire and in which they would not be disturbed. Since Whipsnade first showed the way, many other zoos in all parts of the world have had consistent successes in breeding and rearing bears.

Polar bears have proved more difficult to rear than brown bears, although births in captivity are not infrequent. The sensation caused a few years ago by the successful rearing of

Brumas at the London Zoo will be recalled. Where success has been achieved it seems usually to have been the result of attempts to reproduce the rather unusual natural conditions under which polar bear cubs are born in the wild state. The pregnant female hibernates in the den which she excavates in deep snow, and in this den the temperature rises to as much as 86° F. In these conditions of warmth and darkness the cubs are born, and there they remain for some months feeding from their mother and growing steadily. The provision of similar dark warm dens has been attended with considerable success in several zoos during the past two decades.

The experiences of Whipsnade have provided some interesting and valuable information concerning the problems of building up natural groups of animals exhibiting normal social behaviour. Much of this information has been obtained during the establishment of the various deer herds. It is important to realize that a few animals introduced into a paddock do not automatically constitute a natural group. In the establishment of such a group, there are a number of essential requirements. None of these, however, can be accurately defined, although a fairly good indication of them can be given. In the first place the accommodation provided must be satisfactory, both as to area and surroundings, so as to enable the particular species to settle down naturally. Whipsnade paddocks, for example, provide conditions which are sufficiently like those under which deer live in the wild state to enable them to do so.

With all social animals, the next consideration is the minimum number of individuals that will behave as a natural group. A single pair of deer will certainly not constitute such a group, though they may breed. No precise figures can be given, but the history of the Whipsnade deer herds suggests that half a dozen individuals probably represent the very minimum for the establishment of a natural group. A further factor is the sex ratio within the group. One or two stags and four or five hinds may well become established as a social group, whereas if the sex ratio is reversed no social behaviour will be observed.

The recent history of the red deer at Whipsnade provides some important information on this point. A few years after the last war there were five stags and two hinds. At the rutting season there was no rutting behaviour. It was as though the stags thought it was not worth their while to become excited and quarrel about a couple of hinds. Then the Duke of Bedford presented four pregnant hinds. The effect of this increase in the total number of hinds was sufficient to establish a social group, and in the following autumn full rutting behaviour occurred.

It was one of Chalmers Mitchell's hopes that Whipsnade, and other similar zoological parks which he felt sure would in time be developed on the Whipsnade model, would play a valuable part in the preservation of species threatened with extinction. This hope has already been fulfilled, as we shall see in the succeeding chapters, and without doubt in the future the role of the zoological park in fauna preservation will become increasingly important.

# 5

## The Sea Otter and the Fur Seal

*

Many animals, especially those with some economic value, were hunted with such thoroughness and lack of thought for their ultimate survival during the eighteenth and nineteenth centuries that it was by the merest chance that a few individuals survived into the twentieth century. One of the outstanding stories of ruthless exploitation of a valuable animal is that of the magnificent sea otter (*Enhydra lutris*), a story which has a bright last chapter, because today the animal still lives, having responded to belated protection granted when it was already believed to have become extinct. None was seen for more than twenty years, but today there are flourishing colonies which have developed from the last remnants of the species, remnants which survived unsuspected by man somewhere in the Aleutian Islands.

For the beginning of the story we must go back to 1741. In the early summer of that year an expedition led by the great Russian navigator Vitus Bering sailed from the coast of Siberia to explore the then unknown northern seas. By July they had crossed the sea which now bears their leader's name, and had discovered Alaska. After a few weeks of preliminary surveying they embarked for home, intending to return the following summer. Soon, however, they ran into trouble. In these northern seas there is almost perpetual mist, and they lost their way completely. For weeks they sailed among the uncharted and

76

undiscovered Aleutian Islands, until they were eventually wrecked on the shores of one of them, subsequently named Bering Island. Bering himself had been taken ill during the voyage, and within a few weeks he was dead, victim of the scurvy from which so many of his mariners were also suffering.

Then followed a grim winter spent on the ice-bound and wind-swept island, one of the group now known as the Commanders. For the unfortunate mariners it was a desperate struggle for survival. They ate what they could find. Occasionally a whale carcase was washed ashore, and this kept them going for a week or two. In their dire necessity, however, they made a discovery which was destined to alter the whole course of history in these northern waters. Living among the offshore seaweed beds all around the island, and coming out on the rocks to rest, they found the sea otter. They were indeed the first white men to set eyes on what was to prove the most valuable of all the world's fur-bearing animals.

Their interest in it, however, was as a source of food, and it must have been with a great sense of relief that they discovered that bobrof, the sea beaver, as they called it, made good eating. Through the winter they killed nearly 800 of them, and realizing that the fur was thicker, softer and more luxurious than any they had ever seen, not excepting the fabulous ermine, they saved the pelts in the forlorn hope that when spring came they might somehow be able to make their way back home with them.

The severe winter took heavy toll of their numbers, but as the days began to lengthen and the power of the sun's rays increased, the thoughts of the survivors turned to ways and means of putting to sea again. With timber salvaged from their wrecked ship they managed to improvise a craft which did eventually enable them to transport themselves and their 800 precious pelts back to Siberia.

Their return aroused great interest among the other Siberian mariners, who were not slow to realize the financial possibilities of organized bobrof hunting. Within a few years many ships were engaged on this new fur trade. It was a hard life and a dangerous one, but the rewards were great in a vast country like Russia, where the severity of the winters made the demand for high-quality furs well-nigh inexhaustible.

For more than a century tremendous toll was taken of the sea otters, 3,000 miles of arctic coastline were opened up and came under the dominion of the Russian flag—a whole new empire which owed its origin to this one animal. What was the total otter population along these Alaskan and Aleutian coasts? How many pelts could safely be taken each year without endangering the otter population? No one bothered about these questions. It was sufficient that vast numbers could be caught each year, and no one gave a thought to the possibility that the population might eventually be wiped out. Females and young were exploited as ruthlessly as the males.

How many pelts were shipped back to Russia each year we do not know, but it must have been a large number. Many ships would leave the islands with as many as 5,000 skins as the result of a season's hunting. The numbers of sea otters kept up for a surprisingly long time, but by 1867, when the U.S.A. bought Alaska and its attendant islands from Russia for the comparatively modest sum of 7,200,000 dollars, the vast annual toll had at last begun to show its effect. But if the Russians had paid little attention to the possibility of exterminating the sea otter, the Americans were even less likely to do so. In their own country they were busy slaughtering bison at an almost unbelievable rate, and many smaller animals were also being shot to extinction. Under the new rule, in fact, the sea otter was pursued with renewed vigour, until within a few years a full season's hunting would yield a crew a dozen skins if they were lucky. And of course as sea otter pelts became scarce, so the price soared to fantastic heights, as much as 250 dollars being paid for a single pelt of good quality.

## The Sea Otter and the Fur Seal

It was only the changed climate of opinion concerning conservation in the early years of this century, already noted in the first chapter, which saved the sea otter from final extinction. In 1911 America, Britain, Russia and Japan signed a treaty which covered the exploitation of all animal life in the Bering Sea, and one of its provisions banned completely the hunting of sea otters. This particular clause in the treaty must have seemed almost pointless, because everyone concerned was quite convinced that the last sea otter had already been killed. This belief was strengthened as the years passed by and no reports of living sea otters were received.

In the early 1930's, however, rumours were abroad that at least one small colony of sea otters had survived, and U.S.A. naval and coastguard services received evidence of mysterious visits being paid by Japanese fishing vessels to the Aleutian Islands. It was suggested that they were in fact hunting sea otters. The American Government decided the matter was worth investigating, and in 1936 a naval vessel was sent to make a thorough survey of the area.

The party returned with the good news that a small but apparently flourishing colony of sea otters had been located along the coast of Amchitka Island. Without delay the Aleutian Wildlife Refuge was created as a special branch of the U.S. Fish and Wildlife Service, the body responsible for all matters concerned with the protection of wildlife in the U.S.A., and charged with providing adequate protection for the sea otters. By the outbreak of war they had already begun to multiply, and continued to do so right through the war. Today, thanks to constant vigilance for more than twenty years, it is estimated that the Amchitka population now numbers at least 4,000, and that an equal number of otters are scattered in smaller populations along the coasts of the other islands of the group. The species has thus been saved, and there is every hope that in time it may build up again to its former abundance. It will then be possible for controlled hunting to be allowed, so that the fabulous sea-otter fur can once again take its place in the world's fur markets.

The discovery of colonies has enabled the scientists of the Wildlife Refuge to find out more about the habits of the sea otter, and to confirm accounts which have come down from earlier times. Its habitat is coastal waters where the water is shallow and where there is an abundance of seaweed. Its food consists of various invertebrates which live on these shallow sea beds, the principal item in its diet being sea urchins. The weeds are needed to give the animal protection from the killer whales which are numerous in these northern seas. It spends much of its time lying on its back floating on the surface of the sea, its arms resting across its chest. When it has caught a sea urchin it comes up to the surface, adopts this position, and proceeds to use its chest as a table, placing the urchin on it as it breaks it up with its paws. Seagulls swimming around come in for the scraps which slide off the table into the water. As the otters lie in the water they always seem to be on the alert for the approach of killer whales, easily detected by their large single fins breaking the surface of the water. Often in this position the otter will shade its eyes from the sun with one of its paws.

The sea otter is the largest member of the Carnivore family *Mustelidae*, which includes the otters, weasels and their numerous relatives. Its dentition is unusual in that the cheek teeth, instead of forming sharp cutting edges as in most carnivores, are flattened to form crushing teeth with which the animal can deal with the shells of sea urchins and molluscs. Full grown, the sea otter is about five feet in length and weighs about 70 lb., which is about four times the weight of a full grown land otter.

The female otter has the reputation of being an extremely good mother. Until her single pup is old enough to fend for itself she carries it about in the water under one arm, swimming on her back. She will play with it among the seaweed fronds, and leave it there in safety when she dives for sea urchins. Even when it is strong enough to swim unaided she still watches over it for some months, showing it how to take cover among the weeds if danger threatens, and teaching it how to catch sea urchins on the underwater rock ledges.

When Bering's men landed on Bering Island in 1741 the sea otter was not the only important animal they discovered. Occasionally they caught another animal with a rich fur, the fur seal (*Otaria ursina*). This animal was not an inhabitant of the island, and those which they caught were swimming past the shore. As the sea-otter trade grew, so the traders became more familiar with this creature whose fur was nearly as valuable as that of the sea otter. But until they could find its real home, where it congregated and could be caught in large numbers, it could not be commercially exploited. For years the search for the summer home of the fur seals went on without success, which did not come until 1786. In that year Gerassim Pribilof, a Russian navigator and explorer, sailed his small ship into the foggy wastes of the northern Bering Sea. Early one June morning an island not indicated on the chart loomed out of the mist. Pribilof landed and named the island St. George. Hardly had he got ashore when he realized that he had discovered what sea captains had been searching for during the past forty years and more, the summer breeding grounds of the fur seal, or sea bear.

An incredible sight greeted Pribilof and his men, the greatest concentration of fur-bearing animals that white man had ever set their eyes upon. For the beaches were covered with countless thousands of seals, all basking in the sunshine. There were bulls, cows and pups, each with just enough room to stretch. There were no signs of human inhabitants on St. George, so Pribilof hurried back to the Russian settlement at Unalaska, where he recruited a band of Aleutian Indians. With these he returned to St. George, where he left them to kill and skin seals until he returned.

So persistent were the mists in this part of the world that it was not for another year that the settlers on St. George saw looming out of the mist a second island some thirty-five miles to the north-west. When they investigated this island, which they named St. Paul, they found that it was even more heavily populated with fur seals than St. George.

The prospects here for the fur traders seemed even greater than those offered by the sea otter, and many of them transferred their activities. The next twenty years saw the greatest mass slaughter in the whole history of the fur trade. Despite the millions of seals there were on the beaches of St. George and St. Paul when they were first discovered, they had within twenty years been reduced to such an extent that they were threatened with extinction. In 1806 all killing was halted for two years in an effort to avert catastrophe. After this seal hunting continued for nearly thirty years before a second crisis threatened in 1834. This time the Russian authorities worked out a plan which they thought would safeguard the fur seal against further danger of extinction. From now on, they decreed, only mature bulls could be killed, thus leaving plenty of females to breed and plenty of pups to grow to full size.

They had in fact discovered the principle on which modern exploitation is based, and for the next thirty years the trade flourished without endangering the seal population. In 1864 the total population was estimated at between two and three million, from which an annual harvest of between 80,000 and 90,000 bulls was taken without affecting the strength of the breeding stock.

When America bought Alaska and the islands from Russia in 1867 there was a temporary increase in the numbers of seals killed, which might have endangered the stock once more. Fortunately, however, the American traders relied upon the native Aleutian population to kill the seals for them, and the habit of killing only males had become so well impressed upon them by the Russians in previous years that it still persisted.

In 1870 the American Government granted exclusive rights to kill seals to the Alaska Commercial Company, limiting the number they were allowed to take to a quota of 100,000 each year. For the next ten years or so this number was taken without reducing the total size of the population, but early in the 1880's the numbers began to fall once more. This time, however the fall had nothing to do with the legitimate killing. During the previous years pelagic sealing had developed. Other companies which had no official permit had developed a new technique of shooting the seals on the high seas, where no regulations could operate, and this proved a wasteful method of hunting, for two reasons. Only about one in every five of the seals shot was recovered, the rest sinking to the bottom of the sea before they could be secured. Also when a seal was swimming in the water it was impossible to tell whether it was a male or a female, so that as many females as males were killed. Each cow killed meant the loss of two seals, the cow itself and its pup, which was either left to starve on the shore or was as yet unborn.

This pelagic sealing led to a great deal of ill feeling between U.S.A. and Britain, because British and Canadian sealers were mainly responsible for the wasteful pelagic sealing. At one stage an international crisis threatened when the American authorities seized a fleet of Canadian sealers in the Bering Sea. The trouble started in 1890, and was not finally settled until the treaty of 1911, already referred to. One of the provisions of this treaty was that all pelagic sealing should cease. This left the control of the fur seal herds in the hands of the U.S. Government, who at once put conservation measures into practice. As with the sea otter, the treaty came just in time to prevent the final extinction of an important species. In 1910, in contrast to the hundreds of thousands of pelts taken in earlier times, the total catch was only 12,000 pelts, and a few more years of uncontrolled sealing would undoubtedly have wiped out the stocks.

A survey after the signing of the treaty estimated the total population of fur seals to be in the region of 125,000 animals. As a first measure all killing was suspended for a period of five years to enable the stocks to recover. When killing was resumed in 1917, only three-year-old bachelors, that is males without a harem of cows, could be killed, and as a result of this decree the fur-seal population gradually increased. Each year the number of elegible bachelors killed exceeded that of the previous year, and in 1943, for the first time since 1899 the total harvest exceeded 100,000 skins. Today, thanks to the foresight of the authors of the 1911 treaty, the fur seals have regained something of their former abundance. So numerous are they, and so concentrated on the breeding ledges, that an accurate estimate of the total population is virtually impossible, but reliable authorities put the total today well in excess of three million. Thus through the 1911 treaty two very important animals had been saved from almost certain extinction.

Along with the sea otter and the fur seal, Bering's men discovered a third important animal when they were shipwrecked on Bering Island in 1741, the giant or Steller's sea-cow, and although this animal did become extinct subsequently, it is sufficiently important to be mentioned here. Bering had taken with him a distinguished German zoologist, George Wilhelm Steller, who was able to write a full report on this amazing animal and its habits. The only other members of this most peculiar family of aquatic mammals surviving in the world were the manatees of the river estuaries in tropical America, and the dugongs inhabiting shallow coastal waters in many places from East Africa right across the Indian Ocean to some of the Pacific islands, and extending as far south as northern Australia.

## The Sea Otter and the Fur Seal

Full grown these sea-cows average some six feet in length, but Steller's sea-cow really was a giant, twenty-five to thirty feet long and with a weight of up to four tons. Steller was at a loss to place it, because he was apparently ignorant of the existence of dugongs and manatees. It was therefore a complete mystery to him, and he could only report that it was not a whale and not a seal, leaving others to determine its place in the animal kingdom.

In structure and habits this giant sea-cow was very similar to the manatees and dugongs, and being very easy to catch it provided the marooned sailors with a plentiful supply of meat. When the Aleutian fur trade began in earnest a few years later the sea-cow continued to be a main source of meat for the hunters while they were on the island, with the result that by 1770 the last one had been killed.

No other naturalist had visited Bering Island in the intervening years, so Steller's account is the only one we have on this remarkable animal. For a long time many zoologists were inclined to doubt whether it had ever existed, suspecting it might have been a product of Steller's imagination. All doubt was settled, though, when in 1883 an American scientist, Dr. Stejneger, paid a visit to Bering Island and was able to collect a number of skeletons. These proved not only the earlier existence of the sea-cow, but confirmed Steller's estimate of its size.

Nevertheless the northern sea-cow remains a mystery. Where did it originate, and why, when it was discovered, was it confined around the shores of one small island? Why, too, was it found so far north in such a cold climate, when sea-cows as a group seem to be essentially tropical animals? These questions will in all probability never be answered. Steller's sea-cow could have been a survivor from a remote past when the Aleutian Islands and Alaska basked in sub-tropical sunshine. Surely in any case it must have been much more widespread at one time. One can only assume that the Bering Island population represented the last remnants of the species, extinction having overtaken it elsewhere some time before. That this particular population had not subsequently recolonized the coasts of other island groups is understandable. Sea-cows do not venture far from the shore, and in this area in particular, infested as it is with killer whales, any individuals which took to the open seas would stand little chance of surviving.

If we turn from the far north to South Georgia in the Antarctic we find a similar history of ruthless exploitation followed by recovery after the introduction of protective measures. When Captain Cook discovered South Georgia in 1775 he found there vast herds of fur seals and elephant seals, and from a few years after their discovery until today these herds have formed the basis of a considerable industry. The first commercial visitors were two American sealers who called at the island in 1790 and obtained cargoes of fur-seal skins. From then on the industry grew rapidly, and already by 1801 thirty-one vessels were visiting the island, and the fur-seal rookeries were showing signs of serious depletion. At this time a single vessel often returned to America with more than 50,000 skins. By 1822 the fur seals were rapidly becoming extinct, and for the next hundred years the species hovered on the brink of extermination. As soon as their numbers showed any signs of increasing so the sealers again turned their attention to them, until their numbers had once more become so small that it was not worth while hunting them.

As the fur seals vanished, the sealers turned their attention to the elephant seals. These were valuable not for their skins but for the large amount of oil which could be extracted from their thick layers of blubber. The earlier sealers had found it more profitable to confine their attentions to the fur seals, for it was much easier to club and skin these than it was to flense and boil down the elephant-seal blubber. The usual practice was to put a team of men ashore together with equipment for boiling the blubber and to call for them and their accumulated stocks of oil some months later. In time the elephant seals were also drastically reduced in numbers, but since they were not so commercially valuable as the fur seals they were never brought quite to the same perilous state.

By the time that the whaling industry was being established in South Georgia from 1904 onwards it was believed that the fur seal was already extinct, and the elephant seal was certainly not very plentiful. The new British administration at once proceeded to lay down a series of regulations designed to conserve the stocks of elephant seals and to preserve the fur seal, if in fact any still existed. Killing of elephant seals could henceforth only be carried out by possessors of the necessary license, and in any case only adult males could be killed. Certain areas were set aside as reserves where killing was prohibited and the seals could breed unmolested. From 1910, when the first license was granted, nearly a quarter of a million elephant-seal bulls have been taken, and have yielded about 80,000 tons of oil.

Today the total take is carefully regulated from year to year, the average number allowed being 6,000. Occasionally this figure is raised if it seems that the stock can stand a temporary increase. The coast of South Georgia is divided into four divisions for sealing and two reserves where all killing is prohibited. Each season only three of the divisions are worked, the fourth being given one year for recovery. In each division the average age of the kill is determined each year by means of teeth samples. If the average age of the seals killed in any division shows a decrease this indicates that the population is decreasing, and in following years the numbers permitted to be killed in this division are reduced. When the average age shows an increase there is a corresponding increase in the number which can be taken. With such careful regulation the future of the elephant seal is assured, and the sealers are probably getting the maximum possible harvest.

## The Sea Otter and the Fur Seal

After nearly sixty years of total protection the fur seals of South Georgia are showing a steady increase in numbers. Today the total population is estimated at about 15,000, based on a pup count of 4,500. Nearly all of these are found on Bird Island at the extreme north-west of South Georgia, and it is hoped that in the not too distant future these seals may gradually recolonize much of the mainland coast. No plans for exploiting this population have been made, but it is confidently expected that at some future date, probably during the next decade, controlled fur sealing will be allowed, when of course the number taken will be so regulated as to allow a continual gradual increase in the total population until this has reached its peak. This southern fur seal, incidentally, is a distinct species from that of the Pribilof Islands, though it is similar in general size and habits.

# 6

## *The Last Wild Horse*

★

One day early in January 1900 the Trans-Siberian Express came to a halt at a remote railhead in the heart of Siberia. From it two travellers stepped out into a bleak and inhospitable countryside covered with a thick blanket of snow and swept by cruel icy winds. Worse conditions under which to undertake a journey on foot could hardly be imagined, but the two men had little time to lose. A thousand miles to the south, across uninhabited trackless desert, lay Mongolia, a country which was in those days as remote and inaccessible as anywhere in the world. The small Mongolian township of Kobdo was their ultimate destination, and unless they were there by early spring they would be too late.

So without delay they set out. For nigh on three months they trudged through deep snow and suffered almost unendurable cold, the thermometer often registering more than 80° of frost. Frostbite was a constant danger. They were strong men in the prime of life and quite used to hardship, yet though they pushed themselves to the limits of their physical endurance they were often able to cover no more than ten miles in a day. But they made their objective in time. One day in late March, when the rigours of the continental winter were being softened by early spring sunshine, they walked into Kobdo.

These two men had endured these many weeks of hardship and privation, not in the interests of war, nor in the search for gold or precious stones, but in the interests of science. They had come all the way to Mongolia to search for horses, some of which they hoped to take back to Germany with them. These were, as might be expected, very special horses.

For the beginning of the story we must go back twenty years. In 1881 a Polish explorer, Count Przewalski, returned to Europe after a journey that had taken him right across Mongolia. Here he had discovered a new kind of horse, which he claimed was a genuine wild horse, one of the ancestors from which the domesticated breeds had been derived in very much earlier times. The importance of Przewalski's discovery, if his claim was true, lay in the fact that it was universally believed by zoologists and naturalists that all the wild species of horse which had roamed the plains of Europe and Asia in prehistoric times, and from which the domesticated horse had been derived, had all become extinct hundreds if not thousands of years earlier. It was at least certain that all the so-called wild horses then known in the world were feral, that is they were descended from domesticated horses which had escaped and successfully established themselves in freedom at some time or another in the past.

There had, however, been earlier evidence of the possible existence of a living genuine wild horse. This had been gathered by a British Colonel, Hamilton Smith, while serving with the army of occupation in Paris in 1814. Here he had met some Cossack officers who were well acquainted with Mongolia, and they told him of a wild horse living there which they said was not feral. On his return to London, Hamilton Smith published an account of what he had been told. 'It does not appear', he wrote, 'that the Tahtar or even the Cossack nations have any doubt upon the subject, for they assert that they can distinguish a feral breed from the wild by many tokens; and naming the former Takja and Muzin, denominate the real horse Tarpan and Tarpani. We have had some opportunity of making personal inquiries on wild horses among a considerable number of people from different parts of Russia.

'From the answers of the Russian officers of this irregular cavalry we draw the general conclusion of their decided belief in a true wild and untameable species of horse, and in herds that were of mixed origin. The Tarpan form herds of several hundred, subdivided into smaller troops, each headed by a stallion; they are not found unmixed, excepting towards the borders of China; they prefer wide, open elevated steppes, and always proceed in lines or files, usually with the head to windward, moving slowly forward while grazing, the stallions leading and occasionally going round their own troops; young stallions are often at some distance, and single because they are expelled by the older until they can form a troop of young mares of their own.'

Hamilton Smith's account was in fact an accurate description of the Mongolian wild horse, but at the time of its publication no one seems to have taken it seriously, and naturalists continued to believe that no true wild horse had survived anywhere in the world.

Przewalski did little more than focus attention on the problem, for he had not been able to bring home with him more than a skin, which of course was insufficient evidence either to prove or disprove his claim. Although he did not know it, however, he had obtained this skin from the very area where the Cossack soldiers had told Hamilton Smith that their wild tarpan could be found.

Przewalski's account of his new horse aroused the interest of zoologists everywhere, and of course everyone wanted to see one of these horses in order to determine whether it was a true wild species. But to obtain live specimens from so remote a country was not an easy matter. That a group was finally brought to Europe was due to the Duke of Bedford. He decided that he would like to found a herd at his famous animal park at Woburn

Abbey, so he commissioned Carl Hagenbeck to obtain some for him. Hagenbeck, in addition to his other valuable work, had founded and built up the largest animal collecting business in the world. If he could not obtain an animal, then it was almost certain that no one else could do so. Hagenbeck realized that to fulfil this order would probably be the most difficult task he had ever accepted.

In his book *Beasts and Man* he deals at length with the expedition which eventually succeeded in bringing the Mongolian wild horse to Europe. 'Attempts had often been made before to secure this animal,' he wrote, 'but, with one exception, they had all miscarried. This exception was in the case of the famous naturalist Falz-Fein, who had brought some individuals of this rare species from the steppes of Asia to his estate in the Crimea. Little, therefore, was known about the wild horse; its distribution, its habits, the best mode of capturing it were still unstudied. The conduct of the expedition was entrusted to Wilhelm Grieger, one of my most reliable travellers. On him fell the responsibility of making the preparations for the journey, and afterwards of leading the expedition into Mongolia. He was provided with plenty of money, and also letters of introduction and safe conduct from the Russian Government, the Chinese Ambassador in Berlin, and Prince Alexander of Oldenburg.

'The first thing to be done, however, was to pay a visit to Falz-Fein in south Russia, in order to ascertain from him where these wild horses were to be found. This Grieger did; but he found Falz-Fein reluctant to divulge the information he required. By indirect means, however, Grieger succeeded in ascertaining that the horses were to be found in the neighbourhood of Kobdo, a town situated under the northern slopes of the Altai Mountains—a very long journey right through Russia and western Siberia, into Mongolia.'

Hence it was that Grieger and one companion found themselves tramping through the Siberian winter in the early months of 1900. When they finally arrived in Kobdo they found the local tribal chiefs extremely helpful, and from them they gleaned enough information to enable them to draw up a plan of campaign. Although they were quite unused to the idea of hunting animals in order to capture them, the tribesmen nevertheless volunteered to help them. So it was that by the beginning of May, when the foals were becoming sufficiently independent to be safely separated from their mothers, Grieger had an army of enthusiastic Mongolian tribesmen ready to help him.

The actual story of the capture of the wild horses and their transport back to Europe is best told in Hagenbeck's own words. 'As compared with the prolonged preparations which were necessary,' he wrote, 'the actual catching presented but little difficulty. The method employed was that which has generally been used when young animals are to be caught. It is a habit of the creatures to rest for some hours during the daytime in the vicinity of the drinking place. The Mongolians were instructed to seize this opportunity of stalking them with their own horses. Then at a given signal the whole company break into shouts and yells; and mounting their horses dash upon the herd. The latter spring up in alarm and gallop off into the steppes, leaving behind them nothing but a cloud of dust. The Mongolians give chase, and after a time brown specks are seen at intervals in the dust-cloud. As the chase continues the specks become larger and turn out to be the foals, which are unable to keep up with the older members of the herd. When at last the foals are quite worn out, they stand still, their nostrils swelling and their flanks heaving with exhaustion and terror. All the pursuers have then to do is to slip over their necks a noose attached to the end of a long pole, and conduct them back to camp. Here there are in readiness a number of tame mares with sucking foals, which are requisitioned as wet-nurses for the new arrivals. In three or four days the foster-parents and their young become quite friendly.

'So easy did the Mongolians find this horse-hunting, when

once they had been shown the way, that they went out to do some catching on their own account, and before long no less than thirty foals were secured in the camp. This placed Grieger in some difficulty. The order, which he had come to execute, was only for six. Ought he, then, to incur the additional expense of bringing home thirty? There was nothing for it but to telegraph home to find out. His journey to the nearest telegraph office and back took him over more than a thousand miles of country, and involved him in an absence of three weeks from the camp. When he arrived back, armed with permission to bring the lot, he found that the industrous Mongolians had increased the number to fifty-two. With these the long journey home was commenced, the party consisting not only of the wild foals, but also of their foster-parents, the animals carrying the travellers and their baggage, and thirty native recruits. Slowly the caravan wound its way over hill and dale, in rain and sunshine, in heat and cold. Anxiety for the safety of the captives was never absent. Many of them, as was inevitable, died on the journey, in spite of all the care that could be exercised. And in other ways the journey was decidedly eventful.

'Before many days were passed the first incident occurred, namely, the escape of the camels, owing to the carelessness of the attendants; and it was only with great trouble that their recapture could be effected. The attendants turned out to be a bad set; for after a few weeks Grieger noticed that they were becoming discontented. At last a deputation approached him and announced the intention of the entire company to throw up the work and abandon the caravan, saying that the way was too long, the journey too difficult, and making many other similar excuses. The money, paid them in advance, they would as conscientious men return. In vain did the traveller use all the arts of persuasion to induce the people to remain. In vain did he point out to them that the caravan would be totally lost if they were to desert him at this moment. At last the leaders of the mutiny professed themselves ready to remain, if a rise in salary were granted to them. As soon as Grieger discovered that the whole affair was merely a vulgar attempt at extortion, he changed his tactics. Seizing his Kirghise whip, he promptly proceeded to distribute the augmentation of salary asked for, but in heavy blows instead of coin! This treatment was immediately successful, the mutiny calmed down, the ringleaders begged for pardon; and before long the caravan was jogging merrily along again, without the desertion of a single man. In all, the transportation to Hamburg took eleven months. Out of the fifty-two wild horses which had started, twenty-eight arrived safely at their journey's end, where they were henceforth placed upon a diet of hulled oats, warm bran and carrots. Thus ends the story of how wild horses first came to Europe.'

I have dealt at length with this journey because it is one of the epics of animal collecting, and from the standpoint of fauna preservation perhaps the most important journey ever made. Although Hagenbeck did not know this when he wrote his book in 1909, Grieger's twenty-eight horses were destined to be the only specimens ever to reach Europe. The fate of the wild herds, so plentiful when both Przewalski and Grieger were in Mongolia, is a complete mystery. Sometime after Grieger's visit they must have begun to die out, for in another twenty years they could no longer be found. What had happened to them no one knows. So it came about that the few survivors left in the world today are all descended from the original twenty-eight, with possibly a small contribution from the two mares and a stallion which Falz-Fein had managed to obtain.

By 1950 Przewalski's Mongolian Wild Horse (*Equus caballus przewalskii*), now generally recognized as the last true wild horse left in the world, could claim the sad distinction of being the world's rarest wild mammal. The total world population consisted of two small herds, each about a dozen strong, at Prague and Munich Zoos, an old pair, which had never bred, at

Whipsnade, and one old male, the last survivor of the herd which had flourished for many years at Woburn. With its death in 1955 the Woburn herd came to an end after fifty-four years.

In 1953 the Zoological Society of London decided that the time was ripe to add the Przewalski horse to the growing list of rare animals at Whipsnade, and in January 1954 Mr. E. H. Tong, the Whipsnade Director, went to Prague in order to negotiate the purchase of a young pair, which it was hoped might become the foundation stock of another herd. The pair settled in well at Whipsnade, and a foal born in each of the years 1956 and 1957 gave every hope that Whipsnade would succeed in building up the world's third herd. More recently a few other pairs of wild horses have been sent from Munich and Prague to zoos in America with the hope of building up further breeding herds.

Przewalski's wild horse is an attractive animal about the size of a large pony. Its colour is dun, and it has a relatively large head. The muzzle is whitish and the tips of its ears and the lower parts of its legs are black. It has an erect mane which does not grow forward to form a forelock. During the autumn a long surcoat develops, so that during the winter the horse has a rather shaggy appearance. In the spring this extra coat is shed, leaving only the beautiful sleek undercoat.

Until comparatively recent times a second wild horse, similar in size and general appearance to the Mongolian wild horse, lived in Europe. This was the tarpan, and we know now that it still existed in the Ukrainian steppes during the first half of the nineteenth century. Unfortunately the scientists of the time failed to realize that it was a genuine wild species, believing it was just another feral horse, so no efforts were made to preserve it, and it drifted to inevitable extinction by about the middle of the century. The tarpan had the short bristly mane characteristic of all wild horse species, including the zebras, whereas wild domesticated horses always have long flowing manes, and also show a variety of colouring which is never shown by genuine wild horses.

The tarpan had been the subject of one of the most interesting breeding experiments ever undertaken. About thirty years ago two distinguished German scientists, Heinz Heck, director of the Munich Zoo, and his brother Lutz Heck, director of the Berlin Zoo, began their now famous breeding back experiments, during the course of which they have resurrected two extinct European wild animals, the tarpan and the aurochs. Their experiments were based upon the fact that many of the existing ponies of Europe must have been derived in part at least from the wild tarpan. Thus, they argued, the heritable constitution of the tarpan still existed. Their experiments were designed to pick out the tarpan characteristics from various European ponies, and then to try by cross breeding to combine them in one stock. One difficulty which they had to overcome was that no domestic or feral pony had retained the short bristly wild type mane, so to get this into their experimental stock they had to cross with a Przewalski stallion, and then breed out the qualities which belonged to the Przewalski and were alien to the tarpan.

In his book, *Animals My Adventure*, Lutz Heck describes the brothers' breeding back experiments, and explains the principles on which they were based. 'We proceeded from the principle that no animal can be extinct whose heritable constitution still exists. This constitution may be crossed with other species of animals, it may have suffered changes through race formations, but it still lives, and with the aid of our present-day knowledge of heredity it can be brought back as a whole. Crossings can be bred out again, changes of race can be corrected by suitable selection. In this way animals may reappear after disappearing for centuries. Extinct animals can live again!'

He then goes on to quote an account by Heinz of how they managed to solve the problems of breeding back the tarpan.

## The Last Wild Horse

'There are large numbers of races of horses that are direct descendants from the old forest horse—the Nordic, medium-sized horses, the so-called Scandinavian ponies, the Iceland ponies, the horses of Gotland, the wild horses of Dartmoor, and the so-called Koniks, the farmers' horses in Poland, Galicia, and the Border States. These show the type of the forest horse most clearly. A crossing of these races together would probably not bring us very close to our goal, although it might bring some interesting results. But we thought we might not obtain enough characteristics of the wild animal, as some of those of the domestic animal, for instance the long mane, are common to all these races in the same degree. Accordingly my brother and I pursued another method, based on experience acquired by our father in the Berlin Gardens during his long career there, and since confirmed many times. If an ibex is crossed with a domestic goat, it is a strange fact that the offspring shows not only the colour of the ibex, that of the domestic goat, and intermediate colours, but suddenly the colouring of the wild ancestor of the domestic goat, the Bezoar goat or paseng, although the colour of the wild animal has not been seen in our domestic goats for many generations. This result is rather remarkable. To put it into generally intelligible terms, it seems as if the inheritance of the ibex from the wild animal compels the domestic goat to recall the original characteristics of the wild animal of long ago. The heritable constitution has to decide one way or the other. We did the same thing in breeding back the mouse-grey primeval wild horse living in the forests, the Tarpan. We put stallions of the other type of primeval wild horse, the russet horse of the steppes, to the tame descendant of the mouse-grey Tarpan, with Iceland ponies and Konik mares, and in the second breeding series in Munich there already appeared a fabulous foal! As a young animal it was of an almost uniform grey, with a black mane and black tail and a broad black stripe along the backbone. And when it changed colour it acquired a white underside, dark fronts on the legs, and all the other markings which the old Teuton horse is known to have had—we already had our first primeval horse! An animal had been born which no man had ever hoped to see. That sort of thing is like a fairy-tale, only very much more exciting.'

One very interesting point emerged as the new herd of bred-back tarpans grew. Although no deliberate attempt had been made to produce any special type of hoof, it turned out that the hooves of the new race were much harder than those of any domestic or feral breed. Even the hard hoof of the wild ancestral horse had been achieved. Just after the last war one specimen travelled about 1,000 miles by road harnessed to a cart, and although it was unshod the hoofs were still in perfect condition when it arrived at the end of its journey.

The Heck brothers' breeding back experiments raise an interesting problem. Can we accept their resurrected tarpans and aurochsen as genuine, or are they, as it were, mere copies? It is a difficult question, but at least it can be said that the new animals would probably be identical in appearance with the original wild species. Of course extinct animals can only be recreated in this way if they have been used in the development of domestic breeds. Most wild animals have no domestic counterparts, so for the majority of the large number of species which have become extinct there is no possibility of resurrecting them by breeding back or by any other method.

# 7

## The Problem of Asia's Rhinos

*

Of the five surviving species of rhinoceros, three belong to southern and south-western Asia, and two to Africa. These latter, the so-called white and black rhinoceroses, are still fairly numerous, though fears have been expressed that unless more positive steps are taken to ensure its survival, the white rhinoceros may be faced with the threat of extinction in the future. The Asiatic species, however, all occupy places high up on the list of animals which are rare and in need of special protection if they are to survive for much longer.

The story of the efforts which have been made in the past half century to save the Great Indian One-horned rhinoceros (*Rhinoceros unicornis*) from the very verge of extinction is one of the classic examples of how an animal can be saved through the creation of a nature or game reserve, given adequate legal protective measures.

Several centuries ago the Indian rhino is known to have been common and widespread throughout northern and north-western India and neighbouring countries, but by the early years of this century it had disappeared from most of its former territories. Only in Bengal, Assam and Nepal did it still survive, and there only in very small numbers. In 1904 it was estimated that about a dozen individuals remained in the Kaziranga district of Assam, and the survivals in Bengal were probably fewer than this.

# The Problem of Asia's Rhinos

The reasons for this decline in the rhino populations over the centuries were several. Rhinos were commercially valuable creatures. Almost every part of the animal could be sold, including the meat, which Brahmans were permitted to eat. All kinds of articles were made from the hide, and even the urine of the animal was credited with antiseptic properties. The really valuable part of the animal, however, was the horn. Throughout the East, and particularly in China, it was in great demand on account of its alleged properties as an aphrodisiac. Even in recent times as much as £100 could be obtained for a single horn. The nineteenth-century vogue for 'sport', which often meant shooting as many animals as possible in the shortest possible time, was another formidable hazard which the dwindling rhino populations had to face.

By its habits the rhino played into the hands of its enemies. It is a rather slow and clumsy animal, devoid of any cunning even in the face of danger, and extremely conservative in its movements about its territory, always tending to use the same mud wallow and the same place to perform its toilet. Thus the man with a gun only had to wait near a mud wallow or a heap of dung to be fairly sure of claiming a victim.

The commercial rhino catchers often captured the animals in pits, which were dug along the regular rhino tracks and carefully camouflaged. Bamboo spikes fixed to the bottom of the pit impaled the rhino as it crashed through the unstable top. When the hunter returned it was an easy matter to despatch the unfortunate animal and remove any parts for which he had a market. Sometimes if he was in a hurry, he merely hacked off the horn and left the rhino to die.

These direct attacks by the sportsman and the commercial hunter were not the sole cause of the rhinos' decline, however. Man's activities had an indirect effect on their distribution, and on their numbers. Their habitat is open savannah covered with tall elephant grasses. With the development of agriculture during the past few centuries vast areas formerly covered with this type of vegetation were cleared and given over to cultivation. At first this revolution in agriculture was confined mainly to the fertile lowland plains, so the rhinos retreated to the hill country, where for some time they were safe from this form of human competition. Later, however, man began to open up the hill areas too, converting the wild country into tea plantations and paddy fields. Even in uncultivated districts the grasslands became gradually replaced by woodlands which were of no use to the rhinos. Before the arrival of the farmers the hill tribesmen used to set fire to the grass in order to encourage young growth, and this had the effect of preventing young trees from becoming established. When these tribesmen were driven away, however, the firing ceased, and enabled the trees to grow up and replace the grass.

It was the sudden realization, at the beginning of this century, that the Great Indian One-horned rhinoceros was all but extinct, which stimulated the authorities to take desperate measures in an attempt to save the species. The animal was accorded absolute protection, and a number of areas where it was still known to survive were designated forest reserves. These were later to become game sanctuaries. The most important of these was the Kaziranga Reserve, which became the Kaziranga Game Sanctuary in 1926. It is twenty-five miles long, with a maximum width of eight miles, and occupies an area of 166 square miles, bounded on the north by the Brahmaputra River. For the past three or four decades this has been the home of half of the total world population of the Indian rhino. Had the attempt to preserve the rhino not been successful here it is extremely doubtful if it could have survived anywhere else.

At its foundation in 1908 the Kaziranga Sanctuary is believed to have contained not more than a dozen specimens, but so successful were the protective measures that their numbers increased steadily, until by 1930 the population was estimated to be not less than 150. Then followed an intense wave of poaching, for rhino horn had become even more valuable on account of its scarcity. Measures taken by the Indian Government in 1935, however, succeeded in reducing poaching to an insignificant level, and the rhino population soon increased beyond the 1930 figure. By the early 1940's the numbers may have been as high as 400, but then the rhinos suffered a further setback. The principal cause of this second reduction in the population was mainly due to disease, believed to have been contracted from the domestic cattle and buffaloes belonging to the native populations surrounding the sanctuary. In 1944 the bodies of twenty-two rhinos which had died from some unidentified disease were found in Kaziranga, and in 1947 the bodies of fourteen victims of anthrax were found. The difficult nature of the country makes it unlikely that all the rhinos which died were discovered on either occasion.

Since then various measures have been undertaken to reduce the risk of rhinos being killed by disease contracted from domestic cattle. In December 1951 a team of thirty-one staff and students from the Veterinary College of Gauhati toured the area surrounding the Kaziranga Sanctuary and innoculated about 50,000 domestic cattle against rinderpest, to which the rhinos are susceptible. Poaching has been made more difficult by the creation of a buffer zone surrounding the boundaries of the sanctuary, in which all shooting is prohibited. For some time now poaching has virtually ceased, only one or two rhinos per year at the most falling victim to the poachers' guns.

The latest reliable estimates of the rhino population in India gives the total at something approaching 400, of which 260 are in the Kaziranga Sanctuary. The majority of the remainder are in other sanctuaries in Assam and Bengal.

Outside India the only other areas where the Great Indian rhinoceros still survive are in Nepal. In contrast to the accessibility of the Kaziranga and other Indian sanctuaries containing populations of rhinos, those of Nepal are in isolated and almost inaccessible country. As a result it is extremely difficult to arrive at any reliable estimates of the populations in these areas, or for the authorities to exercise much effective control over poachers. Estimates in fact have varied from fifty, given a few years ago by Mr. E. P. Gee, one of the leading authorities on the Indian rhino, who has played a leading part in its preservation in Kaziranga, and 1,000 given in 1953 by the Forest Department of Nepal.

The replacement of the former aristocratic government by a more popular democratic one has had the effect of stimulating poaching activities, because its protective measures have not been so strictly enforced as those of its predecessor. In 1954, for example, the Nepalese Department of Defence, which is now responsible for their protection, reported that seventy-two rhinos had been killed by poachers during that year, and the figure may well have been higher. If this rate of reduction were to continue for many years the rhino would soon become extinct in Nepal, even if the initial population was 1,000.

During 1958 a disturbing report was received by the International Union for the Conservation of Nature that a band of Indian poachers had entered the Rapti Valley, principal stronghold of the rhino in Nepal, and had killed every rhino they could find. The number of rhinos killed was said to be in the region of 500. Arrangements were made between the Union and the Government of Nepal for Mr. Gee to visit Nepal in order to report on the rhino situation and to make recommendations for the preservation of the Nepalese populations. His report, published in August 1959, gives an estimate of 300 for the total rhino populations of Nepal, and also makes various recommendations for establishing additional protected areas and extending others. The International Union has recommended the report to the Government of Nepal.

The Great Indian One-horned rhinoceros is the largest of

the three Asiatic species. Full-grown specimens may attain a length of at least fourteen feet, a shoulder height of six feet, and a weight of two tons. The horn, which is quite different from the horns found in any other mammals, consisting of a compact mass of horny fibres representing modified hairs growing out from the skin of the snout, is short and thick at the base, and usually quite blunt. It seldom exceeds a foot in length. The hide of the Indian rhino has a much neater appearance than that of the two African species, being divided into sections by folds, and looking rather like armour plating, complete with round marks which look like riveting.

Essentially a grazing animal, the rhino prefers the young grass shoots which grow up after the tall elephant grasses have been burnt, and in the Kaziranga Sanctuary about a quarter of the grass is burnt each year to encourage new growth. Besides providing plenty of food for the rhinos this burning also produces clearings in which visitors to the sanctuary can see the animals. The sanctuary has been open to the public since 1937.

Contrary to popular opinion, the Indian rhino is not generally a ferocious, bad-tempered creature. The majority can be followed up and approached quite closely on the back of an elephant. The occasional individual may charge, but usually proves to be a female with a calf at heel. Elephants, though, all show a natural fear of the rhinos, and those used to carry visitors in the sanctuary have to be carefully trained, a process which may take anything up to eighteen months to complete. Even then some of them will bolt if a rhino does charge. In attacking elephants or other members of their own kind the rhinos do not appear to use their horns. Instead they make very effective use of their well-developed lower incisor teeth. With an open mouth and a vigorous toss of the head they can open long gashes along the sides of their opponents. Although tigers are occasionally reported to attack young rhinos, it is believed that they are afraid of the adults. Man, it seems, is the rhinos' only real enemy.

## The Problem of Asia's Rhinos

By the end of the last war the Kaziranga population seemed so well established that it was considered that one or two young ones could be spared each year to send to zoos in various parts of the world. Although the species was now unlikely ever to become extinct in the wild state, and need to be preserved in captivity, the possibility of an epidemic outbreak could not be completely ruled out. To build up the necessary experience to maintain captive breeding stocks would be a cautious insurance against any serious depletion of the wild populations.

Accordingly in 1947 the Kaziranga authorities made their first attempts to catch young rhinos. They aimed to capture a young pair which they had promised to Whipsnade. The method used is the same as that which the hunters perfected before the days of protection. Camouflaged pits five feet wide, five feet deep and nine feet long are dug along some of the main rhino tracks. Each morning these are inspected. When a young specimen is found in a pit, one end of the pit is dug away to form a ramp down which a wheeled cage can be lowered. When the rhino has been enticed inside and the door made secure, elephants are used to draw it back to camp. Here the captive is released into a small stockade. The first objective is to get the rhino used to human company, and this is achieved by hand feeding through the bars of the stockade. In the majority of cases the young animal loses its fear of man and becomes quite tame within a few days of capture, after which time its captors can enter its cage at feeding time.

The method was first tried out in February 1947, and on the very first night a young male and a young female were trapped. The male, Mohan, was soon tamed, and arrived at Whipsnade during the summer. The female proved a more awkward captive, and unfortunately died of blood poisoning before she had become tame. The Kaziranga staff have found from experience that females tend to be more difficult to tame than males. In most years since 1947 at least two young rhinos have been captured and sent out to zoos, so that today many zoos have a pair from which they are hoping to breed.

Whipsnade had to wait until 1952 for a mate for Mohan, who by this time had settled down and was a well-grown specimen. He had proved a very good-tempered animal. Keepers could enter his paddock freely, and special visitors were even allowed to ride on his back on occasion. Mohini, as the young female was called, settled in equally well. To begin with the two were not allowed in the paddock at the same time, for Mohan was much bigger than his future mate, and it was feared he might attack her. By this time Chicago had had a young pair for four years, and all attempts to introduce them to each other had ended in failure, because every time they met furious fighting broke out, and they had to be separated.

Mohan, however, took a great interest in Mohini and, it seemed, a friendly one. Eventually, after Mohini had had a chance to grow more, they were at last allowed to meet. Fortunately there were no signs of trouble, and the two have lived amicably together ever since. Little was known at this time about the breeding habits of the Indian rhino. Mating had only been observed on a few occasions in the Kaziranga Sanctuary, and only one birth in captivity had ever been recorded. This occurred at Calcutta Zoo on 9th October 1925. Mating had taken place towards the end of March 1924, so the gestation period on this occasion had occupied rather more than eighteen months.

With several zoos each possessing a pair of Kaziranga rhinos, there was of course a good deal of friendly rivalry to be the first zoo to produce a calf. Success was first achieved towards the end of 1956 by Basle Zoo, to be followed by the birth of a calf at Whipsnade in 1957. In 1959 these two young rhinos were sent to Milwaukee Zoo, in the U.S.A., where it is hoped they may eventually breed in their turn.

Compared with the other two species of Asiatic rhinos the

Great Indian rhino must be regarded as a safe species. The Javan rhinoceros (*Rhinoceros sondaicus*), also known as the Lesser One-horned rhinoceros, is very similar in appearance to the Great Indian rhinoceros, but is on the average a slightly smaller animal. It has very similar folds in its skin, with the slight difference that the fold just in front of the shoulder continues right across the back, whereas in the larger species it fades out over the back of the neck.

In earlier times the Javan rhinoceros was very widespread, having a much greater range than the Indian species, extending from northern India and southern China right through southeast Asia to Sumatra and Java. Today it is believed to be extinct everywhere except in Java, though it is not impossible that small populations may still exist in some inaccessible areas. Even in Java, where it was at one time common throughout the island, it is now confined to one small game reserve. As with the Indian species, the spread of agriculture and the commercial value of the animal, and in particular of its horn, both contributed to its downfall.

Serious attempts to preserve the remnants of the species date from 1921, when the Netherlands Indies Government set up the Udjung Kulon Nature Monument, which ten years later became a game reserve. The main purpose of the reserve was to provide a region where both the Javan rhinoceros and the Javan tiger might escape the threat of extinction which hung over them. The Udjung Kulon Reserve is a peninsular which forms the western-most tip of the island. It is thirteen miles long with a maximum width of seven miles, but the neck of land connecting it to the rest of the island is little more than half a mile wide. The total area is 117 square miles, consisting of lowland forest, mostly very dense, interspersed with a few small areas of open pasture land. In order to give the rhinos the best chance of building up a flourishing population, human settlement within the reserve was forbidden, even the staff of the reserve living on the mainland. Constant patrols are maintained by the rangers and wardens, for such is the commercial value of the rhinos that only constant vigilance will protect them from the poachers.

An accurate figure for the total population is even more difficult to obtain than it is for the Indian rhino, but estimates vary between two dozen and eighty. Little is known of their habits, but they are known to frequent wallows. With the strict protection which they now enjoy, it seems reasonable to hope that they are safe from extinction. If they do not survive it will probably be for biological reasons rather than through persecution. The present numbers may be so small that they are below the critical level for normal breeding. From the evidence of the Indian rhino over the past half century in the Kaziranga Sanctuary it would seem that two or three dozen individuals are sufficient as a nucleus stock from which to build a flourishing population, but it is not entirely safe to assume that what is a satisfactory number of animals with which to start building up one species will prove equally so for another, even if it is a closely related one. Whether the present remnants of the Javan rhinoceros in the Udjung Kulon Reserve are enough as a basis for rebuilding the species only the experience of the next two or three decades will decide.

Of the three Asiatic rhinos the one most likely to become extinct in the near future is the Sumatran rhinoceros (*Didermocerus sumatrensis*), also called the Asiatic Two-horned rhinoceros. This is the smallest of all the five existing rhinos, and like the two African species it has two horns. Its maximum dimensions are a length of nine feet and a height of four and a half feet. The front horn rarely exceeds a foot in length, while the hind one is usually only two or three inches long. Seen at a distance, therefore, this species can easily be confused with one or other of the one-horned species. For this reason inexpert reports of any of the three species are always subject to some doubt.

## The Problem of Asia's Rhinos

The original distribution of the Sumatran rhino was similar to that of the Javan rhino. Its range extended from Bengal and Assam right through Burma to Sumatra and Borneo. Today it is still widespread, but in most localities where it occurs the numbers are only small. It is in fact difficult to arrive at any reliable estimate of the total population of the Sumatran rhino today, because it is a much more wary species than the Indian and Javan rhinos and is more at home in dense hill forest, which makes it much more difficult to detect. However, although it probably no longer exists in any part of India or China, small numbers are still believed to inhabit remote forest areas in Burma, Thailand, Cambodia, Laos, Viet Nam, Malaya, Sumatra and Borneo. A full-scale investigation would be necessary to determine the present status of the species, and for most of the areas mentioned almost nothing is known about the numbers of individuals involved, though these are almost certainly small. Only from Burma are there any firm figures, and here the number of rhinos in 1959 was given as about forty.

The total number of Sumatran rhinos still living is almost certainly much greater than the number of surviving Javan rhinos, but they are in much greater danger of final extinction than the latter, because the Javan rhinos all live in a relatively small and effectively protected area, whereas the Sumatran rhinos are scattered over a very wide area, where effective protection is virtually impossible whatever legal protective measures may be decreed. The most urgent need to ensure the survival of the Sumatran rhino is a limited area containing sufficient numbers to ensure adequate breeding and to make effective protection possible.

All three species have suffered in the past and still suffer from the belief in the medicinal and magical properties of various parts of their bodies. Lee Merriam Talbot, an American naturalist working on behalf of the International Union for the Conservation of Nature, has recently made a thorough survey of the Asiatic mammals which are in danger of extinction, and in his report he summarizes the present state of the market for rhino products. He found that with the exception of a few hill tribes, all the peoples of south and east Asia still shared the belief that all parts of the rhino body are valuable. Even in 1955 he found that tiny tubes of rhino urine, presumably collected from zoo rhinos, were on sale in Calcutta. Prices offered for whole rhino bodies or their horns varied from country to country. Peak prices seemed to rule in Sumatra, where a Chinese syndicate were prepared to pay almost £1,000 for a large horn. With such prices as these at stake the problem of conservation is a very difficult one, and it is easy to understand why the poachers are prepared to take risks in order to catch any rhinos which are reported to them.

Although as yet their position is not so critical as that of the Asiatic rhinos, the wild elephants of Ceylon are also today facing a crisis. All the elephants of Asia belong to the same species, *Elephas maximus*, but there are several well defined races, each with its own particular qualities of ability and temperament. For centuries the elephants of Ceylon have been regarded as the most valuable of all the races, with a high reputation for their docility, intelligence and loyalty to their owners when tamed. They have always been in great demand with Indian Princes and Rajahs, who preferred them to the native Indian race. So far there have always been enough captured in Ceylon to satisfy all these demands.

The present danger to the future survival of the Ceylon elephants is due in the main to the expansion of agriculture. While there was extensive jungle there was plenty of room for the elephants and little temptation for them to visit cultivated areas where they might be shot. For some time, however, and particularly since the war, great tracts of forest have been felled and ploughed up as agricultural land. As a result many of the elephant herds have become isolated in comparatively small pockets of jungle completely surrounded by cultivation. Unfortunately no one apparently thought of leaving strips of forest that would have served as corridors through which the animals could have passed from one pocket to another in search of food and water.

As the elephants have become more confined in this way, so their excursions into cultivated areas have increased. The planters of course cannot be expected to put up with the very extensive damage that the elephants do without taking active steps to deal with them. And so they are being shot at such a rate that could very well lead to their extinction in the not too distant future. For the Ceylon elephant to disappear would be a great misfortune, not only from the general standpoint of fauna preservation, but also because of its value as a working animal.

Unfortunately there is no official policy as yet for dealing with this elephant problem, but Major A. N. Weinman, director of the Zoological Gardens at Colombo, has evolved a method which could save the bulk of Ceylon's trapped elephants from destruction. His idea is to capture the elephants and transport them to areas where there is still plenty of jungle for them to roam in without having to make excursions into cultivated estates.

To capture and transfer elephants is not an easy matter, but Major Weinman has already shown that it can be done. He has had valuable allies in this work. Living in the northern parts of Ceylon are the Pannikans, a race of people who for centuries have been noted for their prowess at capturing elephants. They are a fearless and courageous people, able to track elephants through the thickest jungle with uncanny accuracy. So confident are they of their ability to avoid danger, despite the risks that their work involves, that they seldom carry firearms with them.

A working party contains about a dozen hunters, whose equipment consists of a few fire crackers and ropes of deerhide, each consisting of at least seventy-five thongs of hide twisted together. These are immensely strong, a single one being capable of holding a full-grown elephant for a time, but they are also very flexible.

The actual capture of an elephant exercises all the Pannikans' powers of jungle craft. They must creep up to a herd without being detected, and decide which animal they are going to capture. Two of them then work their way right up to the hind legs of the selected animal, carrying with them one end of the hide rope in which a noose has been tied. Others are in readiness to tie the other end firmly to a tree. When all are ready, the noose-bearers await their opportunity to slip the noose over one of the elephant's hind legs before making a dash for safety, and at the same moment the other end is secured to the tree. The remainder of the party are not just idle spectators. It is their job to throw fire crackers and shout at the rest of the herd, causing them to panic and stampede, leaving the captured elephant to its fate. If they were not dispersed they might well come to its aid, and this could be very unpleasant for the hunters.

This is not the end of the dangerous work, for hide ropes have now to be attached to the elephant's other hind leg, both forelegs, and round its neck, and this is no easy task when the elephant is already in a bad temper at having been caught. As soon as possible the captured animal is led to a temporary camp, where it will remain for a time while it gets used to captivity. Each night fires are lighted all round the camp to prevent rescue attempts by the remainder of the herd. Fortunately no other wild animal gets used to captivity as quickly as the elephant, and within a few days it can usually be led quite safely out of the jungle.

The first attempts to transfer elephants have been made on a herd estimated to number between eighty and ninety animals. This herd became isolated in an area of jungle adjoining the Ruaneliya Estate, situated some seventy-five miles from Colombo. The damage they did on the estate was so widespread that the owner was forced to take action. He hoped that shooting a few of the herd might discourage the remainder, and perhaps persuade them to break out from their jungle pocket and seek refuge in some more extensive forest area. Within a year twenty-two had been killed, but the herd unfortunately showed no signs of moving away. It was then that Major Weinman came to the rescue, armed with a permit to capture as many of the herd as he saw fit. The latest information is that fifteen elephants were captured in the first operations, and transferred to Colombo Zoo, to be released subsequently in some more suitable area. Major Weinman plans to continue the operations until the whole herd has been removed from Ruaneliya.

While this and other herds may be saved by such individual efforts, it is clear that the future of the Ceylon elephant can only be guaranteed by an enlightened official policy of conservation which takes due account both of the needs of the elephants and of the farmers. Perhaps it will be necessary deliberately to reduce the total elephant population, but let us hope that it will be possible to provide a permanent area of jungle sanctuary large enough to carry a reasonable number of herds.

Another group of Asiatic animals which have been causing anxiety recently are the various kinds of Chinese and Formosan sika deer. There are several different kinds of sika deer, the best-known and at the same time the least-impressive species being the Japanese sika, which is still quite plentiful and in no danger of extermination. In China, however, there are several different kinds. Opinions differ as to whether these are separate species or merely varieties of the same species. Whichever opinion is correct, the fact remains that each variety is quite distinct from all the others. They are all considerably bigger and more impressive than the Japanese sika, and have very attractive spotted coats.

At one time very common, several factors have combined to reduce them to their present precarious state. They are all essentially woodland animals and all over China and Formosa forests and woodlands have been cut down without any compensating planting of trees. So for a century or more the available habitat of the sika deer has been steadily destroyed, causing a corresponding reduction in the sika populations.

Equally important has been the fact that in Chinese traditional medicine the antlers of sika deer have always played a prominent part. The antlers are cut off before they are fully grown, the velvet stripped off, and the bone thoroughly dried. It is then grated to a powder and made into a soup, and used as a cure for impotence. The velvet is used as a tonic for mothers after childbirth. In order to obtain the antlers the stags are shot, snared or caught in pitfalls. In shooting, the hinds and calves can be spared, but the other two methods destroy these indiscriminately with the stags. High values have been placed on sika stag heads. In 1913 the head of a Manchurian stag was worth between £30 and £40, while in 1929 sika horns in south China fetched as much as £70 a pair. Thus all the sika deer of China have had to contend with both loss of habitat and economic exploitation, and their position today seems to be very precarious.

So long as the Japanese were in control of Formosa the Formosa sika fared rather better, for it was protected by the Japanese, but in the few years since their departure the population has declined almost to the point of extinction.

Although it is very difficult to obtain reliable information about the present state of the various sika deer, it seems likely that they all at least verging on extinction, and therefore the only hope for their ultimate survival may lie in their maintenance in captivity. Fortunately there are herds of the most important kinds living in captivity outside China, and these have assumed considerable importance. There are for example herds of Formosan sika at Woburn, Whipsnade and at the Bronx Zoo in New York, as well as a small but well-cared-for herd in

Japan. Various American and European zoos also have breeding herds of certain of the mainland sikas. Every effort will of course now be made to maintain, increase and divide these herds to ensure the survival of the sika deer at least in captivity if they cannot be preserved in the wild state.

# 8

## Antelopes on the Danger List

*

When the Dutch farmers first came to South Africa they found a bewildering abundance of game. Great herds of grazing herbivores of many different species roamed the vast plains, giving promise of an inexhaustible supply of meat for the farmers and their families, as well as for the native labour they recruited to do their work. Prominent among them—in fact from all accounts more numerous than any others—were the grotesque creatures to which they gave the name wildebeest.

There are two distinct species of wildebeest, or gnu as they are now more familiarly called, the true or white-tailed gnu (*Connochaetes gnou*), sometimes also called the black wildebeest, and the brindled gnu or blue wildebeest (*Connochaetes taurinus*). There is also a variety or sub-species of the latter in East Africa known as the white-bearded gnu (*Connochaetes taurinus albojubatus*). Of the two species, the white-tailed gnu today claims more attention because it belongs to the small but extremely important list of species which have already become extinct in the wild state and are being maintained only in captivity.

The white-tailed gnu is a curious, almost grotesque-looking creature. Although a true antelope, belonging to the same group as the long-faced hartebeests, its antelope affinities are anything but obvious. Its hind end looks very much like that of a small pony, complete with a long tufted tail, while its head and shoulders remind one of a small buffalo. The horns, which in antelopes generally reach skywards, curve downwards to the side of the head, becoming slender as they end in an upward flourish. An unusually wide muzzle is adorned with a fringe of long straight bristles, while a prominent erect mane of stiff hairs completes the picture of a most peculiarly mixed-up animal.

In its behaviour the white-tailed gnu is as eccentric as in its appearance, indulging in the most incredible antics, rather like a four-footed ballet dancer. Gordon Cumming, the famous nineteenth-century hunter-naturalist, has left a vivid description of the behaviour of the white-tailed gnu herds in the days of their abundance.

'Wheeling about in endless circles', he wrote, 'and performing the most extraordinary varieties of intricate evolutions, the shaggy herds of these eccentric and fierce-looking animals caper and gambol round the hunter on every side. While he is riding hard to obtain a shot at a herd in front of him, other herds are charging down wind on his right and left, and, having described a number of circular movements, they take up positions upon the very ground across which he rode only a few minutes before.

'Singly, and in small troops of four or five individuals, the old bull wildebeests may be seen stationed at intervals throughout the plains, standing motionless during a whole forenoon, coolly watching with a philosophic eye the movements of the other game, uttering a loud snorting noise, and also a short sharp cry which is peculiar to them. When the hunter approaches these old bulls, they begin whisking their long white tails in a most eccentric manner; then springing into the air, start prancing and capering, and pursue each other in circles at their utmost speed. Suddenly they all pull up together to overhaul the intruder, when the bulls will often begin fighting in a most violent manner, dropping on their knees at every shock; then, quickly wheeling about, they kick up their heels, whirl their tails with a fantastic flourish, and scour across the plain enveloped in a cloud of dust.'

## Antelopes on the Danger List

Alas, such a sight as this has vanished from the African plains long since, thanks to the Boer farmers. Essentially animals of the open plains of South Africa, the white-tailed gnus were thus most numerous in the areas the Dutch immigrants chose to site their farms. Single herds in those days might well contain several thousand individuals, and the total population of South Africa must have numbered many millions. When grazing they would often associate and mix with herds of quaggas before these became extinct about a century ago, and also with flocks of ostriches. After the disappearance of the quaggas there was an increased tendency to team up with zebra herds for feeding.

Many animals have been exploited by man to the point of extinction because they were particularly valuable to him. The white-tailed gnu suffered this fate through inferiority. As the farms grew, so the number of native labourers increased, as did the problem of feeding them. It did not take the Dutch long to discover that while the flesh of many antelope species was of high quality, that of the white-tailed gnu was inferior and not particularly appetizing. Anything, though, was considered good enough for the labourers, and the better kinds of antelopes too good for them. So while the farmer kept the best meat for himself, and took good care to see that he did not shoot too many of the choicer species to endanger their survival, the gnus were slaughtered indiscriminately.

True, there were so many of them that the possibility of exterminating them probably did not occur to him. No species, though, whatever its initial abundance, is proof against extermination if exploited sufficiently over a long enough period, and as the century drew to its close it became obvious to the Boers that the white-tailed gnu, once the most numerous animal on the plains, was now the rarest of them. In another few years it seemed that the last few survivors must share the fate of their numerous predecessors, and add one more to the growing list of species owing their extinction to man's thoughtless exploitation.

## Antelopes on the Danger List

Not all the farmers, however, were completely indifferent to the fate of their victims, and when they at last realized what they had done an enlightened minority decided that they must take steps to avoid the final consequences of their earlier ruthlessness.

The only hope for the ultimate survival of the species seemed to lie in rounding up the remaining individuals and maintaining them in herds in a state of semi-captivity on some of the larger farms. By 1899 about 500 gnus had been gathered together, and these were divided up into a few large herds and a dozen smaller ones, each one under the care of a farmer pledged to do his utmost to maintain and increase it. As a wild animal the white-tailed gnu was already extinct.

For most species under a threat of extinction 500 protected individuals would be an ample number with which to start consolidating it, but for the white-tailed gnu they proved barely sufficient. Experience with gregarious animals in captivity has shown that there must be more than a certain minimum number of individuals in a herd before an optimum breeding rate is achieved. With some species a pair is sufficient to build up a herd, while with others a dozen or so proves to be a satisfactory number. The experiences at Whipsnade with red deer and other species have already been described. For the white-tailed gnu, however, it seems that only groups containing much larger numbers are able to maintain themselves and show any increase over the years.

As a result today, after sixty years of protection and encouragement, the total world population is little more than double what it was in 1899. There are, however, three large herds, each containing two hundred or more individuals, and the best hope for the future is that these can be gradually expanded to provide, ultimately, herds which can be returned to the wild state in areas where they will not be persecuted.

The experience of Whipsnade, where a small herd has been kept going since 1936, has confirmed the difficulty of maintaining a small group. While herds of all kinds of other gregarious animals have flourished, the white-tailed gnu herd has only managed to hold its own, the rather slow rate of breeding just about balancing the death rate.

Gnus show an unusual temperamental characteristic which adds to the difficulty of herd building. With most herding species additional females can be introduced at any time to increase the breeding potential of a herd. With gnus, however, this is very difficult to do, because the bulls are extremely aggressive towards any newcomers, and are very liable to kill them.

In his book *The Years of Transition*, the late Duke of Bedford, referring to the small herd that was kept at Woburn until the last war, has some interesting things to say about these temperamental difficulties. 'Adult animals which meet as strangers dislike one another intensely, regardless of sex. Some bulls will kill cows and can only be trusted with the latter when they are actually in season. Some cows, if they think a bull is too old, or not sufficiently handsome for them, will combine together to attack him.'

The attitude of white-tailed gnus towards the public, too, is unusual. Whereas most animals in the Whipsnade paddocks get used to the public, and come to the fences either to be fed, or occasionally to charge, the white-tailed gnus prefer to keep as far away from the public as possible, coming near to the fence only when no one is about.

Towards human beings the Duke found the bulls 'hostile and treacherous'. 'Our first bull', he wrote, 'used to feign shyness on most occasions, but at certain times of the year he would wait until one's back was turned and then come up behind one with a sudden fierce rush and, if one turned round, there he was on his knees with his dark eyes blazing and his horns striking the fortunately intervening railings.'

The brindled gnu is if anything more grotesque in appearance than the white-tailed species. It is larger and more thick set, and lacks the grace which offsets the peculiarities of the smaller species. Apart from its different colouring and larger size, it differs from the white-tailed gnu in having an even more elongated face, and horns which are horizontally directed instead of downward sweeping, and are consequently more like those of the buffalo. There is, too, growing down from the throat a long fringe of hair which is white in the white-bearded variety.

Brindled gnus have never been in any real danger of extinction, perhaps because their more northerly distribution meant that they came less into contact with the Boers. In captivity, too, they do well, and show none of the shyness of the white-tailed species. Whipsnade has a small herd of the white-bearded variety, and these will try to charge you through the fence.

The white-tailed gnu is by no means the only antelope to have suffered at the hands of man. Antelopes belong to the great family of *Bovidae*, which includes deer, antelopes and cattle. Whereas deer typically belong to the northern hemisphere, antelopes are essentially animals of Africa and parts of southern Asia. No other whole group of mammals has perhaps been quite so persecuted by hunting. Every species has been drastically reduced in numbers during the past century or so, and others besides the white-tailed gnu have been reduced to the danger level.

Chief among these is the Arabian oryx (*Oryx leucoryx*). In earlier times this species was present in considerable numbers almost everywhere in the Middle East. Unfortunately, however, it was held in very high esteem by the Arabs on account of its great strength and endurance, and it was their belief that by killing and eating it they would acquire some of the oryx's qualities. It was not an easy animal to catch, though, and so long as the Arabs hunted it with their traditional weapons it was not in much danger of extermination. It was the advent of modern firearms, and more recently of modern transport as well, which enabled the hunters to track down and kill this desert antelope more efficiently. Altogether the recent history of the Arabian oryx is a most depressing one, because not only are the authorities in the country where it now survives completely disinterested in whether it survives or not, but even their rulers take part in hunts which can only result in its complete extermination in the very near future. It is only too appropriate that the journal of the Fauna Preservation Society should be called *Oryx*. Certainly the preservation of the Arabian oryx is the most urgent and difficult problem facing conservationists today.

In May 1960 Lee Merriam Talbot, the American naturalist who has been investigating some Asiatic animals on the danger list, published an account of the present state of the oryx population in *Oryx*. It is an antelope of medium size, standing three feet or more at the shoulder, and with a distinctive pair of long, thin straight horns two feet or more in length, those of the female being longer than those of the male. The general body colour is whitish, with brown legs and brown or black patches and stripes on the head. It is essentially a desert species, preferring the gravel plains which are widespread in the Middle East, and particularly in Saudi Arabia. Little is known of its feeding habits, but it is presumed to feed on such annual plants and grasses as it can find. There is a widespread belief among the Arabs that it does not drink, and it has certainly been seen at least 200 miles from the nearest water.

The traditional method of hunting oryx was to follow the herds into the desert on camels during autumn and winter, when temperatures were bearable. The downfall of the species really began when British and American employees of oil companies began hunting in desert cars, and it was not long before the Arab rulers saw the advantage in this method. When the oryx was up against skilled hunters on camels it had a good chance to make its escape, but against the motor-car it was helpless. Motorized hunting became the fashion, and members of the royal family of Saudi Arabia have organized hunting parties in which as many as 300 cars have taken part. This kind of hunting has reached its climax during the last twenty years, and has resulted in the final extermination of all the herds except for one group which survives still in the Rub al Khali desert in the extreme south of the country.

Talbot estimates the remnant population here to number between 100 and 200, but the disturbing feature is that the authorities concerned show not the slightest interest in preserving the species, or of co-operating with those who are keen to do so. Even if there was a last minute change of heart, and the oryx was accorded complete protection, it might well prove impossible to enforce regulations in a remote desert area. The only hope for the survival of this species seems to lie in captivity. Before it is too late, therefore, it must be hoped that sufficient specimens can be captured in Saudi Arabia and transported to suitable zoos where captive herds can be built up. If this programme is successful, the next step should be to release small groups in some area where the habitat is suitable, and where they will not be persecuted. No experiments in herd building in captivity have yet been made, but the few oryx which have been kept in zoos in recent times have all done well.

Allied to the antelopes are an interesting group of creatures called goat-antelopes, which show both antelope and goat features, and form a link between these two groups of the *Bovidae*. In general they are animals of bleak regions, living either in the far north or high among mountain ranges up to a height of 18,000 feet. Most of them have thick hair to protect them from the rigours of the climate, and hoofs which are modified in some way to give them specially sure footing on the mountains.

One species which has suffered at the hands of the hunters, and at one time seemed likely to become exterminated, is the musk-ox (*Ovibos moschatus*). An inhabitant of the arctic wastes of North America and Greenland, the musk-ox bears little external resemblance either to an antelope or to a goat, for it is indeed ox-like in its general appearance and build. This, however, is deceptive, because a study of its internal anatomy reveals features that place it in an intermediate position between the antelopes and the goats.

A full-grown bull stands five feet high at the shoulder and weighs between five and eight hundredweight. The wide flattened bases of the horns meet across the skull, forming a complete shield as in bison and buffalo. As they grow out from the sides of the head they become progressively thinner as they bend first downwards, and then upwards to fairly sharp tips. At their bases they are yellowish-white, gradually darkening along their length until at their tips they are shiny black. Female horns are much smaller, and do not meet across the forehead.

Although the musk-ox is a fairly thick-set animal, with short sturdy legs, it appears to be more massive than it really is by virtue of its extremely thick coat. No animal is better adapted for life on the frozen Arctic wastes, and this coat is one of its important assets. As with all goat-antelopes that have to endure intense cold, it consists of an outer layer of long hair and an inner layer of wool. The outer hair is long and chocolate coloured, curly on the back and shoulders, but hanging straight down from the flanks to form a heavy curtain reaching half-way down the legs. Beneath is a layer of soft brown wool which becomes very thick in winter. On the shoulders the coat is particularly thick, producing a distinct hump like that of the bison. With the onset of warm spring weather the winter undercoat is shed, falling off in wadding-like masses. At this time the musk-ox has a distinctly moth-eaten appearance.

The hoofs of the musk-ox, too, are adapted to its arctic life. The outer hoof on each foot is rounded, and the inner one pointed. Between them there is a considerable growth of hair which helps to give the animals a firm footing on ice and frozen snow. Despite its heavy build and its short legs a musk-ox can gallop very fast, certainly faster than a man can run. The musk part of the name refers to the musky flavour of the flesh. At the breeding season, too, the males acquire a musky smell.

The musk-ox was first discovered by a young Englishman named Henry Kelsey. In June 1689 he set out northwards with an Indian boy from a newly established trading post on the shores of Hudson Bay. Their purpose was to make contact with Indians living in the area in the hope of persuading them to bring in regular supplies of skins to the trading post. One evening, after they had been travelling for about a fortnight, they saw two large animals in the distance. They looked very much like bison, but it seemed incredible that bison could exist in these frozen wastes. Out of curiosity they stalked the animals and shot one. Kelsey realized he had discovered a new animal, and when he returned to the trading post he wrote a detailed account of it. But no one paid any attention to it, and it was to be another 100 years before the existence of the musk-ox became generally known. In 1795 Samuel Hearne, another employee of the Hudson's Bay Company published a book in which he gave a detailed description of the musk-ox.

In the past the range of the musk-ox extended from Alaska right across the American continent to Greenland, being found as far south as the Hudson Bay area. For about three months during the summer, when the snows melt and there is an abundance of fast-growing grasses and herbage, the musk-ox eats enormous amounts and lays down considerable stores of fat. For the rest of the year it has to draw upon these stores, eking them out with such mosses, lichens and dead grass as it can find by digging down through the snow with its feet. It is believed to be able to locate the position of these plants by sniffing over the surface of the snow.

## Antelopes on the Danger List

Musk-oxen are gregarious animals, mixed herds of between twenty and thirty individuals being commonly formed. They are among the few animals that will combine together in defence against a common enemy, usually a pack of wolves. On being attacked they never attempt to run away, but form up into a tight circle surrounding the calves. As the wolves close in they are received with lightning thrusts of the formidible horns, against which they have little chance of success. If the attackers persist for long, three or four adult bulls may suddenly break away from the herd and charge, causing the wolves to retreat in disorder.

Against human hunters this otherwise useful form of collective security proved a serious disadvantage. Packs of dogs were used to attack the oxen, keeping out of harm's way themselves but driving the oxen into their close defensive formation. It was then a simple matter for the hunters to shoot down the whole herd.

Although quite capable of holding its own against the rigours of the arctic winter and against its natural enemies, the musk-ox was unable to stand up against the determined onslaughts of man, who in the course of little more than a century succeeded in reducing an estimated population of one million to a remnant of little more than 10,000.

Wholesale slaughter by man, which has reduced their numbers to the present low figure, came to the musk-oxen later than it did to many other animals, and really started after the wild bison herds had been wiped out in the 1870's. Bison robes were in great demand for their warmth as rugs in the days when the normal method of winter transport was the horse and sleigh. The disappearance of these bison robes from the market created a demand for the even warmer musk-ox robes. From Greenland, too, large numbers were taken by sealers and whalers, the flesh being shipped to Scandinavia and used either to feed dogs or by fur trappers as bait.

During the past two decades, however, the musk-ox has received long overdue protection, with the result that in certain areas in Canada, where protection is complete, and in Greenland where the numbers killed annually are strictly controlled, it is now increasing steadily. In other parts of its original range it had already become extinct. The U.S. Government, however, is planning to re-establish it in Alaska, so there is hope that eventually musk-oxen may be restored to most of their original range.

We must return now to Africa to consider the present position of another antelope, the red lechwe. This is the typical antelope of Northern Rhodesia, where the bulk of the species lives. Until the 1930's it was quite plentiful, the main population of the Kafue flats at that time numbering some 250,000. Today it is doubtful whether there are more than 25,000 on the flats, and elsewhere there are only a few isolated populations containing a few hundred animals each. Two factors have been mainly responsible for this spectacular decline of the species in about a quarter of a century. One is that none of the typical lechwe territory has been included in any of the reserves which have been set up, so that no protected population exists, while the other concerns the traditional method of hunting the lechwe.

From early times the natives have always held an annual lechwe drive, or Chila as it is called. In this the antelopes are driven by lines of beaters helped by dogs. Until recently the driven lechwe were speared by the hunters, whose main purpose was to obtain meat for themselves and their families, and so long as this method of killing was used the Chila probably did no more than take the surplus population each year. By the 1930's, however, the Chila had become more efficient. Shotguns had replaced the spears, and improved transport had made it possible to sell the surplus meat in the towns, so there was every incentive to kill more antelopes. In an effort to stop the increased killing it was declared illegal to sell lechwe meat, but of course once it has been cut up it is very difficult to identify. It is clear that the position of the lechwe herds must be carefully watched, or the animal may well become extinct in the not too distant future. As with other animals of economic value, it should be possible to arrive at an annual exploitation figure which would not endanger the population while at the same time allowing the natives the benefit of a traditional resource. Lt.-Col. R. A. Critchley, President of the Game Preservation and Hunting Association of Northern Rhodesia, considers that if the number taken were limited to 2,000 each year the red lechwe herds would be able to hold their own, and even perhaps show a steady increase. Such a limitation would not deprive the native of meat for himself, but would of course cut out the profit he now gets by selling his surplus catch in the towns.

Immediately following the last war, attention was focussed on the state of the agrimi or wild goat of Crete. Officers who had fought alongside the partisans during the war reported that the goat was now rare, and in danger of extinction. Accordingly the Fauna Preservation Society, the International Union and other bodies interested in fauna preservation arranged for Mr. Hugh Farmar to go to Crete to investigate its present status, and to make suggestions for its preservation.

In classical times the agrimi seems to have been common throughout the Aegean, and during most of the nineteenth century it was reported as being plentiful in Crete. The turning point in its fortunes seems to have been the year 1897. For some time the people of Crete had been in revolt against their Turkish rulers, and matters came to a head in this year. As a result the great powers sent forces to occupy and pacify the island. With them they brought the modern rifle, which came into the hands of the population for the first time, and when the occupying forces left, many of these rifles were retained by the Cretans. Before this the goats could easily keep out of reach of the muzzle-loading guns in the Mount Ida district at the eastern end of the island and in the White Mountains, but against the rifle the mountains were no defence.

Mr. Farmar found the position of the agrimi as unsatisfactory as had been feared, though it was extremely difficult to arrive at any precise estimate of the present population. Through repeated persecution the goats had become extremely wary, and largely nocturnal in their habits. However it seems likely that the Cretan population does not exceed 100, all located in the White Mountains. On each of two small islands off the coast of Crete there are small populations of perhaps a dozen goats descended from a few specimens introduced at some time from Crete. There also seems some possibility that small populations, also derived from introduced specimens, may survive on two or three other Aegean islands.

The obvious preservation measure would be complete protection of the remaining population in the White Mountains, but the inhabitants of this area are a restless and warlike people from whom co-operation might be very difficult to obtain. Nevertheless it is to be hoped that the area in which the goat still survives, extending for some forty square miles, can be established as a sanctuary for the agrimi, with adequate safeguards. Otherwise the only hope for the survival of the species will lie in protecting and increasing the introduced populations on the other islands, or the maintenance of breeding stocks in zoological parks in other parts of the world.

# 9

## *Père David and His Discoveries*

★

I t is curious that the appointment of a French missionary to China should have resulted in two of the most important natural history discoveries of the nineteenth century. Yet when the Lazarist Mission in Paris decided to open a mission school in Peking in 1861, and chose the young missionary Père David to take charge of it, they were unwittingly providing him with the opportunity to make an immortal name for himself. For Père David during the next ten years was destined to discover two rare and interesting animals, and to assemble one of the greatest collections of Chinese animals and plants ever to be sent to Europe.

Long before he left school young Jean Pierre Armand David had two absorbing interests, natural history and missionary work, and had already decided that work in a foreign mission would give him opportunities to devote his life to both causes. By the time of his appointment to Peking at the age of thirty-five he had established a considerable reputation as a scholar, teacher and naturalist. The French Académie des Sciences realized the possibilities of a naturalist of his calibre going to China, about whose natural history little was known in Europe, and he undertook to collect specimens for the National Museum in Paris during his spare time, the Government agreeing to pay all expenses incurred.

In 1861 his collecting activities were confined to districts immediately around Peking, but in 1862 he undertook a month's journey into Mongolia. From now on he became more and more absorbed in natural history exploration, and before long he was giving up most of his time to it, each year's journey being more ambitious than the last, until he had been over a considerable part of China. After each journey consignments of valuable specimens were sent back to France. Some idea of the quality and importance of his systematic collecting can be gained from the fact that even today the National Museum in Paris has a more comprehensive collection of Chinese animal and plant life than any other museum outside China.

Père David made the first of his great discoveries in 1865, a rare species of deer which now bears his name. A few miles to the south of Peking the Chinese Emperors had their Imperial Hunting Park, a vast area of parkland nearly a hundred square miles in extent and entirely surrounded by a high and insurmountable wall about forty miles long. This park was known to contain large herds of deer, though what species were present was not known, because it was strictly private, and no European or other foreigner had ever been allowed to see inside. Père David was intrigued, and often walked outside the wall, always hoping that perhaps one day he might somehow be able to get a glimpse inside.

His chance came one September morning. Workmen had been busy just outside the wall and there, piled up against it, was a heap of sand they were going to use. No one was about, and it was just high enough to enable Père David to hoist himself to the top of the wall by standing on it. It must have been a thrilling moment for him as he found himself looking at a herd of deer grazing about 100 yards away, and realized that he was not only seeing a new species, but a particularly unusual one.

He at once wrote home to Paris, to Professor Milne-Edwards at the Museum of Natural History, describing his discovery.

'Three miles to the south of Peking there is a vast Imperial Park about thirty-six miles perhaps all round. There it is that since time immemorial deer and antelopes have lived in peace. No European can get into this park, but this spring, from the top of the surrounding wall, I had the good fortune to see, rather far off, a herd of more than a hundred of these animals, which looked to me like elks. Unfortunately they had no antlers at this time: what characterizes the animal that I saw is the length of the tail, which struck me as being comparatively as long as the tail of the donkey, a feature not to be found in any of the cervides that I know. It is also smaller than the northern elk. I have made fruitless attempts to get the skin of this species. It is quite impossible to have even portions and the French Legation feel incapable of managing to procure this curious animal by unofficial approaches to the Chinese Government. Luckily I know some Tartar soldiers who are going to do guard duty in this park and I am sure, by means of a bribe, that I shall get hold of a few skins which I shall hasten to send you. The Chinese give to this animal the name of Mi-lou, which means the four odd features, because they consider that this deer takes after the stag by its antlers, the cow by its hooves, the camel by its neck and the mule or even the donkey by its tail.'

A month or two later he again wrote to Milne-Edwards: 'I have spoken to you of an animal which I discovered in the Imperial Park and which is a reindeer with a long tail, and very big antlers, the female having none, I am told. Up to the present I have taken infinite trouble to procure some skins; I am hoping to get two presently.'

Shortly afterwards a secret meeting was arranged with the Tartar soldiers, and one night the skin and bones of a male and a female were passed over the park wall. Père David lost no time in despatching these to Milne-Edwards. Over the next few years, through the efforts of the British envoy and the French Chargé d'Affaires, a number of live specimens were obtained. Most of these reached Europe safely, so that by 1870 the species was represented at several European zoos.

Little is known of the history of Père David's deer up to 1865, and the origin of the Peking herd is a complete mystery. As a wild animal, it is now believed to have become extinct two or three thousand years ago. Semi-fossil remains show that before this time it apparently roamed wild about the Honan district of China. There are no records to show whether the Peking herd had been maintained through all those centuries, or whether it had been founded more recently from other captive herds through which the species had been preserved. Chinese historical literature offers no help, because there is a complete confusion between Père David's deer and the reindeer. All that is certain is that by 1865 the Peking animals represented the sole survivors of the species.

From 1870 onwards no further specimens were obtained from Peking. The small stocks in the various European zoos were just about maintained by occasional breeding. Then, suddenly, two calamities practically wiped out the Peking herd, and these few zoo specimens became the only living representatives of the species.

The first of these calamities occurred in 1894, when during severe flooding the walls of the Imperial Hunting Park were breached. Most of the herd escaped, and the deer were killed and eaten by starving peasants. Then in 1900 the much depleted herd was virtually wiped out by the foreign troops sent to Peking during the Boxer Rising. A few individuals may have escaped, but these did not survive for long, and within a few years the species had become extinct in China.

It was now that the eleventh Duke of Bedford began his great work of saving the species from final extinction. He realized that under town zoo conditions the deer could not possibly survive for very long, as they would not breed in sufficient numbers. The only hope lay in collecting together the few survivors into a single herd and allowing them to live out of doors with plenty of space. He was able to persuade the various European zoos to let him have their few specimens, which amounted to eighteen in all. These were released first into a paddock, and later into the great 3000-acre deer park at Woburn Abbey. So successful were the initial efforts that by 1914 the herd numbered eighty-eight. Then came war, and with it acute shortage of food, which made it impossible to give the deer any supplementary rations during the winter, with the result that many of them died. Sufficient survived, however, until the end of the war, after which the numbers began to increase once more. By the outbreak of the Second World War the herd numbered about 200, and the losses during it was far less than during the previous war. Within a few years of the end of the war the herd approached 400 head.

In 1943 the twelfth Duke considered the time had come to begin establishing herds elsewhere. Although the Woburn herd was doing well, he feared the possibility of an epidemic which might wipe it out, when forty years of endeavour would be lost and the species exterminated. Accordingly he discussed with the Zoological Society of London the possibility of building up a small subsidiary herd at Whipsnade Park. The society was keen to co-operate, but there were practical difficulties. Père David's deer is a large animal, and adult specimens would be very difficult to catch without injuring them. The only possible course seemed to be to catch day-old calves and send them to Whipsnade to be hand reared. Accordingly in the spring of 1944 two male calves were sent to Whipsnade. Male calves were chosen because if the experiment proved a failure, their loss would not reduce the total breeding potential of the herd.

The experiment, however, was a success, and both were successfully reared. As a result two female calves were sent from Woburn in the spring of 1945 to form, with the two males of the previous year, the foundation stock of what was hoped would be the future Whipsnade herd. On 5th April 1947 the first calf was born. This was an important event, because it was the first birth of a Père David calf outside Woburn for nearly fifty years.

During the subsequent build up of the Whipsnade herd several important points emerged. Stags of all species of deer tend to become aggressive during the rutting season, but their aggressiveness is usually confined to their own kind, their natural fear of man being sufficient to prevent them attacking him. Never had a Père David stag attempted to attack anyone at Woburn, but one of the two Whipsnade stags became extremely aggressive at each rut, and charged the fences of its paddock in an endeavour to reach visitors on the other side. This stag, of course, was one of those hand reared in 1944, and provided another example of the fact that wild animals which are hand reared grow up lacking the normal fear of man which all wild animals show, and consequently have no inhibitions about attacking him.

Once the first subsidiary herd had been established, it was decided that attempts should be made to establish further herds in various parts of the world, so that the species might become as widely distributed as possible. In this further expansion Whipsnade continued to play an important part. Although they now had a herd of their own to look after, the society agreed to take about half a dozen calves each year and to hand rear them until they were grown sufficiently to be sent abroad. As a result small groups of three or four deer were sent out to zoos in various parts of the world to form the foundation stock of new herds. Many of these are now breeding regularly, and the world population of Père David's deer is growing steadily. Perhaps the most important of these exports occurred in 1957, when a London zoo-keeper took four well grown calves to Peking. Thus the species came back home after an absence of nearly sixty years.

## Père David and His Discoveries

With the number of herds and the number of individuals increasing all over the world, it would seem that the species must now be considered safe from possible extinction. There are still potential dangers, however, due to certain peculiarities of the species. While most deer thrive when kept in paddocks and small parks, Père David's deer is not very happy in such conditions. There is a possibility therefore that herds kept in comparative small zoo paddocks may lose their fertility after a few generations. When this happens with other captive animals, the usual remedy is to import a male from another stock. Unfortunately, however, because all the Père David's deer left in the world belong to an extremely inbred stock, the introduction of genuine new blood is an impossibility.

Complete safety for the species may ultimately depend upon its being given free run of a large tract of land where there is plenty of water available. It is very fond of water and mud, and will spend hours standing shoulder deep in water. The late Duke of Bedford records that young stags will on occasion indulge in playing and mock-fighting in quite deep water, apparently quite unperturbed by frequent ducking. The stags like nothing better than to cover themselves with mud. They do not roll in it, as red deer stags do, but use their antlers to dig into it and throw it skilfully over their backs.

Père David's deer is of interest to the naturalist quite apart from the incredible story of its survival. It is rather larger than our own red deer, and more heavily built. In many respects it differs considerably from the other Old World deer, as the Chinese in their 'four odd features' recognize. Although it is now established as belonging to that group, these differences led some earlier zoologists to consider that it was really related to the New World deer. The most significant differences concern the hoofs, antlers and tail. Père David's original observations on the tail have already been quoted. It is indeed much longer than in any other deer species, and ends in a long tuft of hairs.

Most deer have dainty feet terminating in a pair of tiny hoofs. The reindeer is an exception, having a large pair of spreading hoofs which click characteristically when it walks. These have evolved to enable the animal to walk over snow. Père David's deer also has spreading hoofs which click. These are thought to have developed to enable it to walk over swampy ground.

The antlers of typical Old World deer consist fundamentally of two branches, a brow tine in front and a beam behind, which are represented by two knobs when the antlers first begin to grow. In Père David's deer the brow tine develops into a massive branched antler, the beam forming a well-developed branch behind. In all other Old World deer, except the reindeer, the main part of the antler is formed from the beam, the brow tine remaining small and unbranched. Second-year stags grow a single short spike, and the full head is developed at six years old. Antler shedding begins in October, but there is a good deal of variation in the date of shedding from year to year. New antlers begin to grow at once, and may take as long as six months to reach full size, a much slower rate of growth than in most other species.

In the early days at Woburn, adult Père David stags developed a curious habit of growing and shedding two pairs of antlers every year instead of the usual one pair, each pair being smaller than normal. This habit has now practically ceased. The late Duke of Bedford suggested that this abnormality may have been brought about in the first place through underfeeding during the First World War.

The Père David deer rutting season occurs much earlier than in other species, extending from June until August. The young are born correspondingly early in the following year. This has an important bearing on the ability of the species to withstand the winter in temperate climates. Stags, as a general rule, cease feeding when they are in rut, and consequently end up in very poor condition. With most species, the lateness of the rut gives the stags little or no time to recover condition before winter sets in, but the Père David stags have sufficient time to regain strength to face the winter. The calves, too, having been born early, are mostly well grown and in good health by this time.

Three years after his discovery of his deer, Père David set out in May 1868 on his greatest journey, which was to last for two years, and it was on this trip that he made his second momentous discovery. By November he had reached the borders of Tibet, and now embarked on an 800-mile journey through difficult country to reach a missionary centre at Chengtu in eastern Tibet early in January, intending to spend some months there studying the natural history of the district. The missionaries, however, urged him to press on to the mountains and forests of Mu-p'in, a small Tibetan principality eight days' journey to the north-west of Chengtu. Particularly interesting to Père David was their story of a 'white bear' they told him lived in these forests.

Accordingly he made his preparations, and towards the end of February set out once more across the mountains, reaching the village of Mu-p'in on the 1st of March. At once he began to search for evidence of the remarkable white bear. At first he could find no clue to its existence, but on the 11th of March he arrived at a farm where he was to spend the night. And there he saw for the first time a skin of the creature he had come so far to find. It was quite unlike the skin of any other animal he had ever seen, and it was not entirely white, having some prominent black patches.

In reply to his excited inquiries the farmer assured him that the animal did indeed live in the neighbouring forests, and he arranged for local hunters to go out in search of a specimen. One can imagine Père David's excitement when they returned a few days later with a young one. He was not equipped to attempt to carry the animal back to Peking alive, so he killed and preserved it. As soon as possible he despatched it to Paris, where it created tremendous interest among the zoologists of Europe. He was later able to organize the collection of a few living specimens to send home, and for a number of years these were to be seen in the Jardin des Plantes.

For a variety of reasons giant pandas are seldom seen in captivity. They are rare animals, and live in inaccessible forests. An expedition may spend weeks, and even months, hunting for specimens and still have to return home empty handed. They are, too, among the most difficult animals to maintain in captivity, owing to their rigid feeding habits. With most animals whose natural diet is difficult to obtain when they are brought from their native country, it is usually possible to change them over to a satisfactory substitute diet. The giant panda, however, seems extremely reluctant to forsake its rather monotonous diet of bamboo shoots for something which could be more easily provided in a temperate climate.

Only three specimens have ever been seen in Britain, all at the London Zoo. The arrival of the first, Ming, in 1938 created a sensation. To satisfy her needs bamboo shoots were sent up from Cornwall each day, and despite the added difficulties created by the war, Ming survived for six years. As soon as the war ended the Zoological Society made application to the Chinese Government for another specimen. Owing to their rarity giant pandas are strictly protected, but the society's request was sympathetically received, and in due course Lien-ho arrived by air in May 1946. She survived until 1950. After her death the society decided for the time being to make no further attempt to secure a replacement until such time as more had been learned about the giant panda's requirements in captivity.

The circumstances in which the society's third specimen arrived were somewhat unusual. In the summer of 1958 a Mr. Heini Demmer appeared in the country with a giant panda, which he deposited at the zoo for three weeks to give the public a chance to see it. By the time the three weeks were up, however, it was announced that the society had purchased Chi-chi, as the panda was called, from Mr. Demmer. In view of the difficulties which had been experienced with the two earlier specimens, the society asked the authorities at Moscow and Peking Zoos for advice on feeding and other matters, as they were the only zoos with recent experience of giant pandas.

The giant panda in the wild state has a restricted range, being found only in bamboo jungles of the Szechwan Mountains at altitudes ranging from 6,000 to 11,000 feet. So far as is known it feeds on little else than bamboo, holding the canes in its front paws with the help of a special pad developed at the base of the thumb. Bamboo fibres are extremely tough, but the panda has a very efficient dentition, and well-developed masticatory muscles to deal with its rather difficult diet.

Owing to its secretive nature and its habit of lying up in caves, under rocks or even in the forks of trees during most of the day, and also to the great difficulty of penetrating the thick bamboo forests, the giant panda is a most difficult animal to study in its native habitat. It seems to be a solitary animal except during the breeding season, though virtually nothing is known of its breeding habits. It has never bred in captivity, and until more zoo specimens become available captive breeding will remain a remote possibility.

For a long time after its discovery the exact position of the giant panda in the animal kingdom remained a mystery. Many believed that it was an aberrant member of the bear family, and it was often referred to as the parti-coloured bear. Although, however, there are some resemblances, more recent anatomical work has shown that it is not a bear.

It is in fact one of those isolated animals that is not really closely related to any other animal. Anatomically it is a carnivore, though in feeding habits it is herbivorous. Today it is placed in the small family *Procyonidae*, which comprises the racoons (*Procyon* species) and their allies, whose distribution is confined to the New World, the true or Himalayan panda (*Ailurus fulgens*), and the giant panda (*Ailuropoda melanoleuca*), both from central Asia. It is not, however, closely related either to the Himalayan panda or to the racoons, forming rather an intermediate form connecting them with the bears (*Ursidae*).

The *Ursidae* and the *Procyonidae* represent separate offshoots which originated from the true dog family in the Miocene period, and in the further evolution of both families there has been a steadily increasing tendency to develop non-carnivorous habits.

Although there is today only one species of giant panda in the world, fossil remains of a second species of similar size were discovered in a cave in Burma in 1914. This species is believed to have survived until comparatively recent times, and may well have owed its extinction to persecution by man. Nothing, of course, is known of its coat colour or of its habits. Its canine teeth, however, were much better developed than those of the existing species, suggesting that it was at least partially carnivorous.

The true or Himalayan panda is a much smaller animal which is more widespread than the giant panda. Although it was first found in the Himalayas, it occurs also in Burma and in the Chinese provinces of Yunnan and Szechwan. Essentially it is an animal of the mountain forests, being found at altitudes ranging from 7,000 to 13,000 feet. It is not a strictly nocturnal animal, but it does spend much of the daytime curled up asleep among the topmost branches of the forest trees, coming down on the ground to feed on a mixed diet of grasses, roots, seeds and fruits in the early morning and late evening.

The Himalayan panda is sometimes called the cat-bear, and it is indeed similar in size to a large domestic cat. Although it is related, but not closely, to the giant panda, there are some considerable differences between the two animals. For example, the toes of the giant panda are set almost in a straight line, like those of a bear, and the pads beneath its prominent non-retractile claws are naked cushions on which it walks. Much of its time is spent on the ground, where it is very agile. In contrast the Himalayan panda's toes are arranged in a curve, and its claws are partially retractile. The pads are completely covered and hidden by a thick growth of hair. Claws and hairy pads both probably contribute towards its agility in the trees, where it spends most of its time. On the ground it is not a very agile creature.

Although it is the best known, Père David's deer is not the only species of deer to have faced the prospect of extinction in recent times. Three other Asiatic species and one American have caused considerable anxiety to preservationists during the past two or three decades. One of these is the brow-antlered deer, which is also variously called Eld's deer and the thamin. It exists in two distinct sub-species, the Manipur thamin (*Cervus eldi eldi*) and the Burmese thamin (*Cervus eldi thamin*). The former species has never been known outside the Manipur valley, to the north of the Bay of Bengal. It is a deer of medium size, inhabiting open swampy ground. The name brow-antlered deer refers to the fact that the brow tine, instead of projecting horizontally as in most species of deer, curves downwards and outwards just above its eyes.

The position of the Manipur race had been steadily deteriorating until 1934, when it was officially declared a protected animal, and killing was forbidden. Unfortunately, however, effective protection was impossible during the war, when large numbers were killed both by the military forces and by the local villagers. After the war it was for some years believed to have become extinct, and in fact in 1951 the Manipur Forest Department officially declared it to be extinct. Fortunately, however, a few odd pockets had evidently managed to survive, for it was rediscovered in 1952 around the marshy margins of Logtak Lake, and in 1953 an area of twenty square miles was set aside as a sanctuary for it. Latest reports say that here it is steadily increasing, but it is proving very difficult to obtain any reliable estimates of its numbers, because the area of the sanctuary is very difficult to penetrate, which of course may well be a good thing, because it will make poaching activities less possible. In 1956 a pair were sent to Calcutta Zoo, where they are said to be flourishing. As with other species of deer threatened with extinction, it might be a good idea to establish a few captive herds in various parts of the world, just in case the protective measures prove ultimately unsuccessful. It shows one unfortunate trait which makes the task of protecting it more difficult. During the rainy period it takes to wandering, and migrates to drier areas, where of course it is much easier for the poacher to kill it.

The Burmese thamin was at one time extremely common almost everywhere in Burma, but by the outbreak of the last war fears were being expressed for its ultimate survival. During the war the Japanese troops occupied much of its remaining range, and its numbers became seriously reduced. By 1949 it was declared to be one of the animals most in danger of extinction in the world. Since then the thamin has increased steadily, and already by 1956 it was possible for the conference of the International Union for the Conservation of Nature to remove it from the list of species faced with the threat of extinction.

Curious beliefs held by the Burmese people must play a part in helping to reduce the numbers killed. Its hide has no commerical value, and the people believe that eating its flesh causes leprosy. Indeed their name for this disease, translated, means thamin patches. Another afflication attributed to eating thamin meat is venereal disease.

Further north in Kashmir lives the Kashmir stag or hangul (*Cervis elaphus hanglu*), one of the finest species of deer in the world, related to and similar in size and appearance to the European red deer and the American wapiti. Until Indian independence was granted in 1948 the Kashmir stag was in no danger of extinction. It had always been regarded as the property of the Maharajah of Kashmir, and was strictly protected. It lives on the densely wooded mountain slopes, wintering at about 5,000 feet but climbing up to between 9,000 and 13,000 feet during the summer. The disturbed conditions in the Kashmir following independence were disastrous for the species, and by 1952 the numbers had declined to an estimated 325.

Today, thanks to such protection as is possible in difficult country, the numbers are thought to be increasing, and the total population is now reliably put at about 550. The main dangers now are from poachers, who work mainly during the winter when the stags come down from the hills, and the increasing pressure of agriculture and grazing. Many of the farmers have guns for crop and herd protection, and without adequate supervision it is impossible to see that they only use these for legitimate purposes. There is now a sanctuary extending to eighty-five square miles, but the game department of Kashmir, under whose authority it is placed, has insufficient funds to employ enough guards to make an effective control area.

Further north again, in the mountain forests of southern China and Tibet, lives one of the smallest of the world's deer species, a deer with such a price on its head that only its inaccessibility has enabled it to survive. It is the musk deer (*Moschus moschiferus*), from which comes the most sought after and valuable of all perfumes.

Despite the difficulties involved in tracking the musk deer in the dense rhododendron forests in which it lives, the musk hunters pursue them with such determination and skill that the annual toll approaches 100,000. How much longer the species can stand this enormous drain on its numbers we do not know. Protective measures by the governments concerned would have little value, for in these immense areas of wild and uninhabited country it would be quite impossible to enforce them.

All kinds of methods are employed to catch the deer. In the valleys nets are placed across one end, the hunters and their dogs then advancing right through the valley from the opposite end, making as much noise as they can to drive the frightened deer into the nets. In more open country the dogs are used to drive them from cover, when they can be shot either with rifle or poisoned arrow. Others are caught in traps set along well used deer paths in the forest.

Many, however, manage to elude all these methods of capture, and remain hidden in dense thickets. But even they are not safe, for the hunter knows they have one weakness, curiosity and an apparent love of music. So he sits down quietly and begins to play on the flute he always carries with him. The little creature seems irresistibly tempted to investigate the strange sounds, but as he emerges the liquid notes of the flute give way to the deadly crack of the rifle. Only adult males produce musk, but since at a distance there is no way of distinguishing the sexes, neither carrying antlers, males and females are both killed, thus increasing the annual wastage.

Although musk-deer venison is said to be a particular delicacy, the musk hunter is only interested in the little musk pouch, about the size of a walnut, lying at the base of the abdomen. This he carefully removes, and then leaves the carcase to rot. Within the pouch is the granular musk, so sweet yet so strong that anything that comes into contact with it retains the scent for weeks or months afterwards. So valuable is musk that the temptation to swindle is great. Many of the hunters have perfected methods of introducing foreign material into the musk pouch to increase the total amount of 'grain' which can finally be extracted from it, and hence the price that they will get for it. The introduced material soon becomes as strongly scented as the real grains.

Musk grains as removed from the pouches are worth more than £100 per pound, but finally purified musk extracted from the grains can be worth as much as £500 an ounce. The quality of the musk is said to vary according to the area in which the deer live, the most valuable musk of all coming from Tibet.

Musk hunting is clearly a profitable livelihood, but it can also be a dangerous one. Just as there is no law to protect the deer, so there is no protection for the hunters, who are valuable and easy prey for the bandit. For him to pick out those carrying musk is an easy matter, the strong scent giving them away. Many a hunter has been killed for the bag full of musk pouches he has been carrying.

Because of the high cost and the difficulty of obtaining musk and other valuable ingredients of high-class perfumes, chemists have spent a great deal of time trying to replace them with synthetic products. Recently pure musk has been synthesized. This is good news, because it means the end of persecution for the musk deer as soon as the process has been developed on a commerical scale.

At the other end of the world another species of deer has been giving anxiety lately. This is the Florida key deer (*Odocoileus virginianus clavium*), a small species inhabiting the Florida Keys region. In the years following the last war it became increasingly obvious to those who knew the area that the numbers of key deer were falling rapidly, and that it was becoming scarce. As a result of the anxiety expressed by American conservationists the Fish and Wildlife Service appointed an agent in 1951 to make a study of the deer's habits, and try to arouse the interest of the local people in preserving it. He found that the chief cause of the reduction in the population was the large amount of traffic on the roads. Large numbers of deer were killed annually on the main highways. This was an unusual cause of scarcity in a wild animal, and the only possible solution seemed to be to set aside an area of sufficient extent as a refuge for the deer. At this time the total population was estimated to number not more than twenty-five, so any action would have to be taken promptly if it was not to be too late. Fortunately the Americans, by now fully conscious of the need to preserve wild life, did act quickly, and Congress has authorized the establishment of a National Key Deer Refuge. Negotiations are now in hand for the necessary land, which should ensure the safety of the species. Meantime the latest reports suggest that it has fared rather better in recent years, and may have increased to a total of 125 head.

# 10

# The Okapi—Sole Relative of the Giraffe

★

In 1860 Philip Henry Gosse, a leading British naturalist, wrote a book which he called *The Romance of Natural History*. In one of the chapters he discussed the possibility of discovering strange new animals in the hitherto unexplored forests of Central Africa, and suggested that here perhaps might be found the mysterious unicorn. 'It is highly probable that an animal of ancient renown, and one in which England has (or ought to have) a peculiar interest, resides in the region just indicated. I refer to one of the supporters of Britain's shield, the famed unicorn. We may not, to be sure, find him exactly what the heraldic artists delight to represent him—a sort of mongrel between a deer and a horse, with cloven hoofs, a tuft-tipped tail, and a horn spirally twisted to a point; but there may be the original of the traditionary portrait of which this is the gradually corrupted copy.

'Dr. Andrew Smith, an able and sober zoologist, who has investigated with much enterprise and success the zoology of South Africa, has collected a good deal of information about a one-horned animal which is yet unknown to Europeans, and which appears to occupy an intermediate rank between the massive rhinoceros and the lighter form of the horse. Cavassi, cited by Labat, heard of such a beast in Congo under the name of Abada; and Ruppel mentions it as commonly spoken of in Kordofan, where it is called Nillekma, and sometimes Arase—

that is, unicorn. Mr. Freeman, the excellent missionary whose name is so intimately connected with Madagascar, received the most particular accounts of the creature from an intelligent native of a region lying northward from Mozambique. According to this witness, an animal called the Ndzoodzoo is by no means rare in Makooa. It is about the size of a horse, extremely fleet and strong. A single horn projects from its forehead from two feet to two and a half feet in length. This is said to be flexible when the animal is asleep, and can be curled up at pleasure, like an elephant's proboscis; but it becomes stiff and hard under the excitement of rage. It is extremely fierce, invariably attacking a man whenever it discerns him. The device adopted by the natives to escape from its fury, is to climb a thick and tall tree out of sight. If the enraged animal ceases to see his enemy, he presently gallops away; but, if he catches sight of the fugitive in a tree, he instantly commences an attack on the tree with his frontal horn, boring and ripping it till he brings it down, when the wretched man is presently gored to death. If the tree is not very bulky, the perseverance of the creature usually succeeds in overturning it. His fury spends itself in goring and mangling the carcase, as he never attempts to devour it. The female is altogether without a horn.'

The unknown is of course always exciting, and Gosse's book fired the imagination of a schoolboy who read it a few years after it was published. There and then he resolved that one day, when he grew up, he would explore this unknown Africa for himself and try to find the unicorn. Schoolboy ambitions are of course often forgotten, but Harry Johnston stuck to his, and in due course became a very distinguished explorer and administrator in Africa. After nearly twenty years serving in various colonies Sir Harry Johnston, as he had now become, was in 1899 appointed Consul General for the Uganda Protectorate.

Before leaving to take up his new post he called to say goodbye to Sir Henry Stanley, the great explorer. 'If you get a chance,' Stanley told him, 'mind you take a trip into that wonderful Ituri forest, which, I am sure, contains some strange beasts not yet made known to science. You may find there the donkey that the pygmies told me they caught in pitfalls, or you may succeed in getting the huge black pig which I know lives in that forest, for I have seen it on more than one occasion rush past when we were fighting our way through the tangle of undergrowth.'

Early in 1900 Johnston had occasion to rescue some Congo pygmies who had been forcibly captured with the idea of exhibiting them at the Paris Exhibition. They remained as his guests for some time until an escort could be provided to conduct them safely back to their native territory. During their stay he questioned them about the wild donkeys which Stanley had mentioned. 'Dense as the pygmies were on many matters on which they were questioned,' he wrote afterwards, 'they hastened to answer this particular query. They did catch such an animal as I had described in pits, and they called it o'api—one or two said o'ati, which brought the name very near to Stanley's name for it, atti. On asking them what it was like they at first pointed to a tame zebra, and subsequently to a mule, and said it was like a cross between the two, being partly striped, but having big ears like the mule. As to horns, they were very uncertain.'

Johnston travelled with the escort party to the Belgian Congo, and there met two Belgian officials, Lieutenant Meura and Lieutenant Eriksson. They told Johnston that they knew of the animal and had indeed eaten its flesh, though neither of them had ever seen it alive. As to its affinities it seemed to them less like a horse than an antelope, and they were sure that it had more than one toe on each hoof, though whether it had three or two they could not remember. They also thought it had no horns.

The three day search which followed is best told in Sir Harry Johnston's own words. 'I was now eager to start in search of this strange animal, and was duly furnished with guides for the purpose. Seeing how shy the okapi has proved to be, it is possible that in the short space of time at my disposal I might have been no more fortunate in my attempt to shoot one than had been all the Europeans who have followed me in this quest. Still, I spoilt what chances I might have had of seeing, if not shooting, this rare creature, by the prepossession which had now got hold of me that I was in search of a new type of horse, possibly a surviving three-toed horse which had taken to the dense forest in Africa as its last refuge.

'Consequently, when on the second day of our journey we crossed a little stream valley in the dark forest, and saw imprinted in the sand cloven-hoof marks rather like those of an eland, and about the same size, and my native guide excitedly declared I was now on the track of the okapi, as these people called it, I repudiated the idea, saying that these wonderful footprints were either those of a forest eland or a bongo, and that such animals being known I could look for them another day. What I wanted was the imprint of a single hoof.

'They were much mystified, but continued to assert that the okapi had two hoofs like an ox. After three days' journey I came to a halt, because my followers were ill with forest fever. In the village where we rested the natives used as bandoliers for their guns, or additions to their scanty clothing, handsomely marked pieces of hide—brownish black, orange, and creamy white. They at once attracted my attention and seemed to me to be the pieces of skin of an entirely new type of zebra. These, however, I was told, were taken from the okapi whenever it was caught in pitfalls. Everyone being positive as to this, I now believed I held—as I did—portions of the skin of this unknown beast. On returning to the Belgian headquarters at Mbeni my belief was confirmed. The Congo officials told me that I had pieces of okapi skin. They were good enough to promise, as various causes had prevented me from staying any longer, that when the next okapi was caught by their soldiers or native neighbours in a pitfall, they would endeavour to secure the entire skin, and also the skull.'

For the completion of his discovery Johnston was much indebted to Lieutenant Eriksson, who in due course sent him the historic skin and two skulls which established the structure and systematic position of the okapi. Johnston at once recognized the animal as being a relative of the giraffe.

The story continues in London at a series of meetings of the Zoological Society during 1901 and 1902. The bandoliers arrived first, and on the strength of these Dr. P. L. Sclater, who was then the secretary of the society, pronounced the new animal to be a hitherto unknown forest-dwelling zebra, which he named *Equus johnstoni*. When the skulls and skin subsequently arrived, they were examined by Sir Ray Lankester, who confirmed Johnston's identification, and renamed the animal *Ocapia johnstoni*. In recognition of his outstanding contribution to zoology by his discovery of the okapi Sir Harry Johnston was awarded the coveted Gold Medal of the Zoological Society, an award which has been made on only five occasions in a century and a quarter.

At first sight there is little to suggest the okapi's relationship with the giraffe. It does, however, stand significantly higher at the shoulder than at the rear, so that the line on the back slopes upwards towards the front end, as though foreshadowing the more pronounced slope of the giraffe's back. The small horns of the male okapi give a valuable clue to its relationship with the giraffe. The horns of deer, antelopes and cattle all originate as bony growths from the skull. A giraffe's horns, however, arise first as fibrous thickenings beneath the skin over the head. These thickenings soon become ossified as short bony horns quite separate from the skull. Until they finally fuse with the bones of the skull some time after they are formed, they remain freely movable with the scalp. The okapi has similar ossicones, as these horns are called.

# The Okapi—Sole Relative of the Giraffe

The okapi's general structure is, however, very close to that of certain extinct mammals known to be early relatives of the giraffe. This evidence places the okapi unmistakably as the only other living member of the *Giraffidae*. The principal differences betwen the okapi and the giraffe can be related to the very different habitats in which they are found. The giraffe lives in open grass country, browsing on the leaves of the trees which are scattered about. Its colouring blends well with its surroundings, and in spite of its height makes it relatively inconspicuous. For warning of the approach of enemies it relies mainly on its sense of sight. The okapi, on the other hand, lives in the dense forest where little light penetrates, and its dark coat makes it almost invisible against the dark background. It would certainly be a conspicuous animal in open country, as would the giraffe in a dark forest. In the depths of the forest, too, hearing is a more important sense than sight, which accounts for the okapi's large cupped ears. It has been suggested that the whitish stripes across the buttocks and hind limbs may help the animals to follow one another through the dimly lit forest tracks.

The interest aroused by the okapi's discovery resulted in numerous expeditions being sent to the Belgian Congo from all over the world to obtain specimens. As the beast was never plentiful, on account of its persecution by the pygmies, this new danger threatened it with extinction. The Belgian Government stepped in, and at the International Convention for the protection of fauna and flora held in London in 1933 the okapi was accorded total protection. Since that time the capture or killing of okapis has been entirely prohibited, except by the special Groupe de Capture d'Okapis (G.C.O.), a department of the Belgian Board of Agriculture and Colonies. Only a small number are caught annually, and these are distributed to zoos in rotation.

The method used by the G.C.O. to capture the okapi is a

modification of the pitfall method which the pygmies have probably used for several thousand years. Pitfalls are dug along known okapi tracks in the forest, and carefully camouflaged. The okapi being almost incapable of jumping, a pit six feet deep is sufficient to prevent the escape of an animal which averages about five feet six inches at the shoulder. The pitfalls are examined twice a day. When the captured okapi is discovered, the pit is quickly surrounded with a light stockade, on the sides of which bundles of leaves are hung. Earth is then shovelled into the pit until the okapi can walk out and feed on the leaves.

More fencing is then used to enclose a passage about two and a half feet wide running from the enclosure to the nearest cart track, where it runs into a portable transport cage placed on a cart. This passage may be anything up to half a mile long. When it is finally completed the entrance is opened and the okapi walks quietly along it and into the cage, which is then carried back to the camp. Here it is released into a large enclosure where it soon settles down and gets used to the native keepers, who look after it for some weeks. When it is sufficiently tame it begins the long journey to Antwerp Zoo, the distribution centre from which all captured specimens are despatched. It is an interesting commentary on the timidity of the okapi that few Europeans, even those in charge of the G.C.O., have ever seen one alive in the jungle.

Events in the Congo following the withdrawal of the Belgians in 1960 have naturally given rise to considerably anxiety about the future safety of the okapi population. It will be very interesting to see what attitude the Congolese Government adopts towards the preservation of wildlife generally, and towards the okapi in particular. It may well be, as was the case when India was granted her independence, that the new régime will take great pride in its natural heritage, and will want to do all it can to preserve it.

Whatever attitude is finally adopted, however, there must

always be some doubt about whether a small population of animals living in dense forest where really effective protection is virtually impossible, can ever become safe from extinction. Conservationists would feel much happier if small breeding stocks had already been established in a few zoological parks in different parts of the world, as a precaution against the worst happening to the wild population. Little, however, is known about the breeding of okapis in captivity, because each zoo fortunate to be on the distribution list is usually allocated only one specimen. It is to be hoped that before long facilities will be granted enabling at least one or two zoological parks to try to build up captive breeding stocks.

## I I

# *American and European Bison*

*

The seasonal migration of birds, often involving massed flights of a thousand miles or more, are well known. Many fish, too, undertake long migrations at certain times of the year. Among land animals, however, migration is less common, and when it does occur it is seldom spectacular, involving nothing more than a gradual drift northward or southward.

The one great exception was the American bison (*Bison bison*), often incorrectly called the buffalo. In the days of its abundance on the great plains of North America it provided the most spectacular example ever known of mass seasonal migration among land animals. Its later history during the second half of the nineteenth century is an outstanding example of the way in which indiscriminate slaughter could reduce a once abundant animal to the verge of extinction.

When the white man first went to America the bison herds probably represented the biggest aggregation of land animals anywhere in the world. It has been estimated that until well into the nineteenth century there were at least sixty million of them. Every spring and autumn this huge population migrated. As autumn approached they moved southward to avoid the rigours of the northern winter, returning northward again in the spring as the snows were melting.

To have witnessed these vast herds on the move must have been an awe-inspiring experience. 'As far as my eye could reach, the country seemed absolutely blackened by innumerable herds,' runs an account written in 1832 of a journey to the Rocky Mountains. From the same year we have another account: 'Towards evening, on the rise of a hill, we were suddenly greeted by a sight which seemed to astonish even the oldest among us. The whole plain, as far as the eye could discern, was covered by one enormous mass of buffalo.' The writer estimated the area covered by buffalo to measure eight miles in width and ten miles in length. A conservative estimate of the number of animals in this vast conglomeration put it in excess of four millions. The thought of four million animals, each weighing half a ton, all in one great assembly, is staggering!

Stories have been told of the spring migrations developing into stampedes in which hundreds of thousands of bisons were drowned trying to cross the rivers on thawing ice, the dead bodies of the first arrivals eventually damming the river to form a bridge across which the rest of the herd could cross to safety. It is said that many islands in the great Mississippi and Missouri rivers were first formed by piles of bison skeletons. During these spring migrations the Indians killed many bison by driving them over the cliffs.

Before the white man came to the Middle West, the bison was the main economic asset of the Red Indian tribes. From it they obtained almost everything they needed; skins from which they made their homes and their clothing, shoes and bed covering; sinews for bow strings; horns from which they made spoons; and meat, which formed a main part of their diet. They shot the bison from horseback with bow and arrow. The annual toll was great, but it made no more impression upon the herds than did prairie fires and migration disasters, or the depredations of wolves and grizzly bears.

When, however, the white settlers began to push westwards

towards the end of the eighteenth century, the bison as a wild animal was doomed to extinction. Contact with the white pioneers created new tastes among the Indians. They wanted manufactured goods such as steel knives and firearms, and they acquired a taste for whisky. All these things, and many more besides, they could get from the white man in exchange for bison skins.

With their new rifles they were able to kill many more bison than with their traditional bows and arrows. What they did not realize was that in destroying the bison they were risking their own freedom. The white man, however, saw quite clearly that if only the bison could be wiped out, he could starve the Indian into submission.

The Indian alone, however, even with modern firearms, could not really endanger the species, though he did reduce its numbers in certain areas. The events which really doomed the bison was the construction of the Union Pacific transcontinental railway, begun in the 1860's. Great armies of workers had to be fed, and the cheapest way to do this was to shoot the ever-present bison.

As the railroad was opened, section by section, so the professional hunters moved in, slaughtering the bison in tens of thousands, removing the hides and tongues, which were esteemed a delicacy, and leaving the carcasses to rot on the plains. For the tongues and hides, sent back by rail to the big eastern towns, there was a virtually unlimited market. It was as a professional hunter that William F. Cody earned his title of Buffalo Bill. He was one of the most skilled bison hunters, accounting for 4,280 bison in a period of eighteen months. In one day alone he killed sixty-nine.

In little more than fifteen years from 1867 slaughter on an unprecedented scale all but exterminated the bison. Even in 1871 there were still vast numbers left, and in that year at least one herd numbering several million animals was encountered.

But from 1870 to 1875 at least two and a half million animals were killed every year.

So it was that by 1883 only one considerable herd about 10,000 strong remained, in north Dakota. All the rest, apart from small isolated groups, had been wiped off the face of the earth. Even so the hunters could not leave it alone. In September a party set out with the express purpose of annihilating this last remnant of the species, killing more than a thousand bison on their very first day's hunting. By the middle of November their mission was completed, and the American bison as a wild animal had to all intents and purposes ceased to exist.

Almost too late the conscience of the American nation was roused, and the killing of bison was declared illegal. Fortunately a few isolated groups had escaped destruction by retiring to remote areas, and a few far-sighted farmers had captured small numbers of calves, from which they had built up small breeding herds. From these and from other small herds living in a state of semi-domestication in various parks, the species was eventually revived. A census taken in 1889 showed a total estimated population of 541, made up of many small groups scattered through Canada and the U.S.A. Fortunately the American bison is an animal which does well both in the wild and in captivity, and its numbers steadily increased. Today it can be considered completely safe, with a world population probably in excess of ten million. The majority of these are of course still in America, but there are a number of small but flourishing herds in captivity in zoos and parks in other parts of the world.

One of the first, if not the first, bison herds to be established outside America was founded at Woburn about 1910. This has continued to flourish for half a century, and in 1930 eight bison from this herd were presented by the Duke of Bedford to Whipsnade Park while it was still being developed. These were in fact among the first animals to arrive at Whipsnade, and when the park was opened to the public in 1931 Bison Hill soon became one of its major attractions.

Although they do well in captivity, they must be well fed. The late Duke of Bedford has something to say about this, and also about their breeding. 'On the whole they do well when properly fed, but they cannot stand short commons in winter, and a war-time diet, with oat straw instead of hay and no corn, pulls them down badly in condition and checks breeding. There is a well-marked rutting season in August, when the old bulls utter a loud, rolling grunt or bellow. The calves are born in May and June, but an odd one may appear out of season, even in winter. When first born the calves are a light yellowish-red colour but they darken when only a very few months old.' The Whipsnade bison herd suffered considerably during the last war, and breeding ceased altogether. A revival only occurred after new bulls had been obtained from Canada, after which the Whip-snade stock was split into two herds, both of which have now flourished for more than ten years.

One would imagine that an animal as large and powerful as the bison would have nothing to fear from any other animal except perhaps the grizzly bear and the wolf, but apparently this is not so. Again the late Duke of Bedford has some interesting obser-vations based on the experiences at Woburn. 'Latterly the mis-take was made of keeping the wapiti in the same large enclosure as the American bison. This was not at all a good plan as the wapiti stags bullied the bison unmercifully during the rutting season, while the bison drove the wapiti hinds and calves away from the food in winter. An American who had not seen the two animals together might perhaps be in doubt if asked his opinion as to whether a "bull buffalo" or a "bull elk" would prove master in a fight and he might even bestow his verdict in favour of the mighty bovine. Actually the bison hasn't a look in, the big stag's superior activity and formidable antlers giving him every advantage. I have seen a huge master bull bison in

September come bellowing down with his cows, only to be put to instant and ignominious flight by a very second-rate wapiti stag.'

The only close relative of the American bison is the European bison or wisent (*Bison bonasus*). Like the American species it has been reduced from a widespread and flourishing species to a state of near extermination. Indeed its present position is a good deal worse than that of the American species, and although the position has improved somewhat since the last war, it is certainly not yet out of danger.

In general appearance it is similar to the American bison, but is taller and not quite so heavily built. There is, too, not such a pronounced slope from the shoulders to the hind quarters, and the tail is longer and more hairy. The breeding season extends from July to September, and the calves are born in the following spring and early summer. These have the same dark colour as their parents, and are not light in colour like the American bison calves. The cows seem to be very attentive mothers, and tend to keep with other mothers when they have calves. In the wild state this habit would undoubtedly be a valuable safety measure against attacks by wolves. So jealous are they for the safety of their calves that they have been seen to drive off pheasants and jackdaws if these have approached too closely.

In one respect the two bison species differ considerably. Whereas the American bison is essentially an animal of vast open plains, the European bison is a forest species. It seems, however, that they are grazing rather than browsing animals, for although it has been stated that tree branches form an essential part of their diet, the Duke of Bedford and others who have captive herds do not find that they seem at all keen on them. They must, however, be well fed, and have access to good pasture containing a variety of different grasses. In the worst weather conditions they are completely hardy, but they soon succumb to poor quality feeding, a characteristic they share with the American bison.

## American and European Bison

The American bison was reduced to the verge of extinction by the rifle, but the European bison owes its present predicament to quite a different cause, though in both cases man was equally responsible. Until about the sixth century a vast forest covered most of Europe, through which the bison roamed in great numbers. We have no evidence on which to base even an approximate estimate of the total population, but it would certainly not have approached the almost astronomical figures achieved by the American species. From the end of the sixth century, however, the forests began to disappear as agriculture developed, and with the reduction of the forests came a corresponding reduction in the total bison population. Both processes were gradual, and took place over a period of well over one thousand years. Even in the early days the ruling princes in many areas introduced strict laws to protect the bison, death in many cases being the penalty for killing them. This, the earliest example of legal protection of a wild species, was not, however, enacted in the interests of fauna preservation as such. The princes were interested only in maintaining stocks for hunting.

By the end of the eighteenth century the once vast virgin forest had become reduced to a single relatively small forest, the Puszcza Bialowieska, in Poland, extending to a few thousand square miles. In this forest lived the last herd of wisent, variously estimated at this time to number between 300 and 500. Then came the partition of Poland, when the Bialowieska Forest became the private hunting ground of the Tsars of Russia. For more than a century now the bison were to enjoy strict protection, but despite this their numbers only increased slowly. Certainly the hunting parties were not to blame for this, for every care was taken to limit these so that they would not result in excessive depletion of the stock. The reason put forward by the Russian scientists was that the stock itself was declining through inbreeding, which had resulted in a loss of vitality. More recent examination of the condition in the forests during the period have however revealed the real cause of the comparative failure of the bison. They were subject to very heavy competition from vast herds of red, fallow and roe deer, which were also encouraged in the interests of hunting. As a result the bison were hard put to it to find sufficient food. It is true that throughout the winter plenty of hay was distributed through the forest for them, but this was of poor quality and, as already mentioned, the one thing that bison cannot tolerate is unsuitable feeding.

Even so, the species was not really in any danger of extinction before 1914. The First World War, however, was disastrous for the bison. During the first three years of the war, because of inadequate feeding, the numbers were reduced to about 200. This was bad enough, but worse was to come. During 1919–20, when the German armies were in full retreat from the eastern front, they passed right through the Bialowieza Forest, and here they were heavily engaged by the Lithuanians. A little later the forest was the scene of much bitter fighting between the Bolshevic armies and the Poles. When at last peace was restored, not a single bison remained alive in the forest. At this time, too, the last wild bison in the Caucasus was killed. In this area a few hundred had survived on the mountain slopes. And so it was that the sole survivors of the species were those maintained in parks in the custody of private owners, and a few odd specimens in zoos.

At the end of the First World War the European bison was thus near the top of the list of animals in danger of extinction. In 1923 an international meeting was held in Paris to consider the whole problem of the protection of nature. At this meeting Jan Sztoleman, a Polish naturalist, proposed that an International Society for the Protection of the European Bison should be formed, and his suggestion was adopted. The first task of the new body was to investigate the existing herds to determine which were pure bred and which were crossed with the American species, because there had been a certain amount of cross breeding.

The result of all this activity was the publication in 1932 of the first *Pedigree Book of the European Bison*. In this first book only thirty bison were admitted as pure-bred animals, made up of small groups at five breeding centres in Britain, Germany, Holland, Poland and Sweden. The Polish centre had recently been reformed by the transfer of two cows and a bull from the German centre in 1929.

By the outbreak of the Second World War the number of bison had reached nearly 100. The war, however, brought renewed anxiety, because only the Swedish breeding centre remained entirely outside the war zone, although the British centre at Woburn could be considered fairly safe from military danger. In the event the bison fared much better in this war than in the previous one, although there were losses due in the main to inadequate feeding. The first accurate estimate of the post-war population was made in 1947 with a new edition of the *Pedigree Book*. This listed a total number of 98 bison. From then on the population increased slowly but steadily, and by 1955 had again topped the 200 mark. To emphasize that even so the species could not be considered safe from possible disaster, the Polish stocks were almost completely wiped out in 1953 by a severe outbreak of foot-and-mouth disease. However, these herds have now made a very good recovery, and the latest available figures put the total Polish population at something over 100 head. From the existing herds, too, other breeding centres have been established in Russia, Bulgaria, Holland, Denmark, Austria and Czechoslovakia.

As with Père David's deer, the ultimate hope is that small groups can be released in their original natural habitat, so that the species can once more live as a wild population. The first small attempt to restore the bison to the wild state was made in 1952, when two bulls, two cows and a calf were released in the

Bialowieza Forest. So far they seem to have managed well without any special care or feeding, so that there is every reason for hoping that a really large wild population will eventually be built up.

The European bison is another animal which the Dukes of Bedford have played a part in saving from extinction in their 3,000-acre animal park at Woburn. The Woburn herd was founded between the wars. At the first attempt two cows and a bull were imported, but for some reason these did not breed, so a further importation was necessary. Unfortunately accidents seemed to dog the herd during the 1930's, but by the outbreak of war the numbers had increased to more than a dozen. This small group then became potentially extremely important, because it was quite a possibility that war might destroy all the Continental herds. In this event the Woburn bison would have become the sole survivors of the species. Fortunately, as we have seen, the war had far less effect on the bison population than had been feared.

In earlier times a second species of wild cattle roamed the vast forests which once covered much of Europe. These were the aurochsen, the wild ancestors of our domestic cattle. They were magnificent creatures, but wild and dangerous, the great bulls weighing anything up to a ton. With the spread of civilization and the consequent cutting down of the forests throughout the Middle Ages, the aurochsen began to vanish. By the beginning of the seventeenth century only a single herd remained, in the Jaktorowka Forest in Poland not far from Warsaw, and here it was in 1627 that the last aurochs died.

It was in an attempt to resurrect the aurochs that the Heck brothers began their breeding-back experiment in 1921. To produce a new aurochs they had first of all to travel throughout Europe looking at all the primitive breeds of domestic cattle, so that they might assemble an assortment of cattle which would between them show all the main characteristics of the extinct species. Mediaeval drawings and descriptions, skeletons in museums, and cave drawings from earlier times had all contributed information which enabled them to form a picture of what the aurochs really looked like.

Once assembled, the assorted collection of cattle were crossed according to a carefully worked-out plan. Some characteristics had to be bred out, and others accentuated, until gradually all the desired points were being incorporated into a single stock. After more than ten years and the birth of several hundred calves came the exciting day they had been waiting for. One calf was born which, as it developed, showed all the characteristics they had been trying to blend. It was in fact the first of the new race of aurochsen, but its appearance did not mean that the experiment was at an end. Many more years of breeding were necessary before they had built up a complete herd of aurochsen breeding true to type. Today, however, there is such a herd at Munich Zoo, showing both the size and the temperamental characteristics of their wild ancestors.

In Britain today there are five small herds of primitive white cattle which show a clearer relationship to the aurochs than any of our other cattle. These park cattle are often referred to as wild cattle, and some of them may well be genuine wild forms, so little do we really know about the origin of our domesticated breeds. They certainly represent a much earlier stage in the development of domestic breeds than any other cattle.

The most important of these white cattle are the Chillingham cattle, owned by the Earl of Tankerville and kept in his park at Chillingham in Northumberland. This herd has a continuous history since the thirteenth century and the Tankerville family have always been extremely careful to see that no crossing with other cattle took place throughout this time. The park was enclosed towards the end of the thirteenth century, at a time when it is known that there were plenty of white cattle roaming wild in the district. Those left outside the park subsequently disappeared, leaving the park herd as the only survivors. What we do not know is where these Northumbrian white cattle came from in the first place.

If the Chillingham cattle are not a genuine wild herd, it seems likely that their remote ancestors had not been domesticated for long, for their behaviour is in many respects more like that of genuine wild cattle than of a domesticated breed. One bull always manages to establish himself as the king bull, and so long as he is strong enough to withstand their challenges no other bulls are allowed to serve the cows. There is a good deal of challenging and mock fighting, as there is in a deer herd at the rutting season, but serious injury or death seldom result. Domestic cattle generally breed in their first year, but the Chillingham cows are usually three or four years old before they have their first calves, and these are suckled until they are more than a year old.

Twice during its history the Chillingham herd has been in danger of extinction. A severe epidemic in 1760 reduced the herd to a few cows and three bulls, but two of these fought and killed each other. Fortunately the surviving bull was fertile, and the herd was gradually restored by careful management. The second danger period for the herd occurred during the severe winter of 1947, when twenty out of a total of thirty-three died. Again the herd eventually recovered. It would be a great pity if this interesting herd were ever allowed to become extinct, but it would obviously be safer if at least one more small herd could be established elsewhere as an insurance against epidemics or other disasters. The other four herds of white park cattle, the Cadzow, Chartley, Dynevor and Vaynol are all quite small, and less pure bred than the Chillingham, but are nevertheless of importance in the history of the domesticated breeds.

# 12

## Carnivores in Need of Protection

★

Until recently various kinds of brown bear were widely distributed and plentiful throughout the cold and temperate regions of Central Europe, Asia and North America. To the really enthusiastic nineteenth-century taxonomists they provided wonderful opportunities for the exercise of their special talents, and they were sorted and classified into an incredible number of different types. Perhaps the record is held by the zoologist who restricted his efforts to the brown and grizzly bears of the United States and Canada, but who nevertheless was able to produce the astonishing total of eighty-four species and sub-species! Today all the brown bears of the northern hemisphere are recognized as belonging to a single species, *Ursus arctos*, embracing a small number of sub-species. Of these the most impressive is the Kodiak bear, *Ursus arctos middendorffi*. To this bear belongs the distinction of being the largest and, unfortunately, the rarest bear in the world.

Until the 1890's these giant bears flourished virtually undiscovered in the remote and inhospitable island of Kodiak, which lies between Alaska and the far north-west of the American continent. A Russian zoologist, Middendorf, had in fact made brief mention of this bear in a paper published in 1851, but it was left to Hart Merriam, the American naturalist, to investigate reports that a giant bear exceeding all others in size existed in this island. Merriam was able to confirm these reports, and in 1896 he published the first full description of the animal.

Once discovered, the Kodiak bear's very size and power proved its greatest liability, for it at once became target number one for every American game hunter's rifle. The highlight of a shooting career was now an expedition to Kodiak Island. Once there, it seemed a pity to collect one trophy and then depart. Consequently the bears were killed in dozens, with no thought for the future of the species. Within thirty years one of the finest wild animals in the world was rapidly approaching extinction. Then, just before it was too late, the United States Government stepped in, and in 1926 the Kodiak bear was accorded absolute protection. It is much easier, however, to reduce a population of wild animals to a remnant than to build it up again. Although the final annihilation of the Kodiak bear was averted, or at least postponed, there has been no subsequent rapid increase, and today the position of the wild population remains precarious.

Although Kodiak bears are the largest carnivorous animals in the world, they are not exclusively flesh eaters, nor do they rely on large prey. When warmer spring weather brings them out of their winter hibernation quarters in the hills they descend to the plains in the coastal areas, where they feed on young grass shoots for a few weeks. By the beginning of May they have reached the shores of the island, where they pick up a mixed living of dead fish and other animals washed up by the tide, and seaweed.

Besides this mixed and largely vegetarian diet they also eat mice, ground squirrels and other burrowing animals, which they dig out with their paws. The bear, we are told by an observer, 'determines the underground position of a mouse by scent, and digs, sometimes furrowing the earth along the mouse's burrow, until the mouse is exposed, when the bear places its paw over it, and, after biting it in the head, swallows it whole without chewing it. It requires five to ten minutes to dig out a mouse.' Even so, many of the mice are lost.

## Carnivores in Need of Protection

It seems incredible that an animal weighing three-quarters of a ton or more should devote so much time and energy to obtaining so insignificant a morsel. The truth is that until June the bear is not really feeding in earnest. It is at this time that the spawning migrations of the salmon begin, when countless numbers of fish swim into the rivers from the sea to spawn. These provide the Kodiak bear with its real annual feast. From now until late October, when the salmon migration finally comes to an end, the Kodiak justifies its title of 'fish bear'. Forsaking all other kinds of food, except occasional berries, shoots and roots to provide a little variety, it now concentrates for four or five months on intensive salmon fishing.

Seen in a zoo cage, bears often seem rather slow creatures. In this, however, they are deceptive. When necessary they are capable of lightning movements, as occasional rash zoo visitors have discovered when they have reached towards the cage bars to offer food. They have come away with a vivid and often painful impression of the animals' quick ability to snatch. Kodiaks fishing show amazing swiftness of movement. They stand on a rock jutting out over the river, or even wade on a sand bar in shallow water. As the salmon rush past they are hooked out on to the bank with rapid sweeps of the bears' front paws.

Kodiak bears are very strong and have great powers of endurance. With a single blow of their paws they can fell young trees up to four inches in diameter, breaking cleanly through the trunk. On Kodiak Island they move about along well-marked tracks that they have made. These never deviate to avoid steep gradients, and may continue for several thousand feet straight up a mountainside. Along these steep paths and through dense undergrowth they are said to be able to proceed at a bounding gallop for mile after mile without sign of distress, at a speed which in the circumstances would cause a man to gasp for breath after a hundred yards. On level ground they are believed to be capable of approaching thirty miles an hour. There are no other large animals on Kodiak Island against which they could pit their strength, but they would undoubtedly be more than a match for almost any other animal in the world. Their large canine teeth are hardly less formidible than those of the lion or the tiger, while their body weight is several times greater.

Like most bears, Kodiaks in the wild state hibernate during the winter months. As the supply of salmon runs out and the weather gets colder towards the end of October they cease feeding, leave the rivers and migrate inland towards the hills, where they seek out a suitable cave or lair in which to spend the winter. While they have been feeding on the salmon they have accumulated a thick layer of fat beneath the skin, which will serve as an internal food store to tide them over until they begin feeding again in the following spring.

Kodiak bears are essentially solitary animals. Even the males and females take no notice of one another except for a few weeks in July, when they associate in pairs for mating. Cubs are born to the female in late January or early February, while she is in hibernation. All bear cubs at birth are relatively much smaller than the new-born young of most other large animals, weighing only about a pound and a half each. For the first two or three months of their lives they remain in hibernation with their mothers, feeding on her milk and growing apace.

The small size of the cubs is an adaptation to this method of breeding. If the cubs were comparatively as large as the new-born young of other mammals they would impose too great a strain on the mother's resources. In the first warm days of early spring they are brought out for their first airing. By this time they have grown into sturdy youngsters with surplus energy to use up in playing among themselves and in teasing their mothers. Bears kept in captivity in temperate climates do not hibernate, but as a substitute the females always retire to their dens to have their cubs, staying there for some weeks while they grow. Sometimes it is not until they are brought out for the first time six to eight weeks after birth that zoo authorities know how many cubs there are.

Because of their precarious position in the wild state, the progress which has been made in breeding Kodiak bears in captivity is of considerable importance. The story of Kodiak breeding begins in the summer of 1933, when two young cubs were captured in Kodiak Island and sent to the Chicago Zoo. When they arrived there in August they were seven months old and weighed 40 lb. each. Before this only odd specimens had ever been exhibited in captivity. As the pair grew up they mated every year, and one or two cubs were produced on each occasion. None of these survived, however, until the pair born on 8th February 1944. These were successfully reared, and were eventually purchased by means of a generous private donation for Whipsnade Park, where they arrived in 1946.

In January 1947, although she was not yet three years old, the Whipsnade female gave birth to two cubs, which did not, however, survive. For the next six years she continued to produce one or two cubs almost every year, but none of these survived. Sometimes the mother brought them out into the den, and they died of exposure. Even when she kept them inside and fed them they did not grow, and finally died of starvation. Even after a fortnight they were no bigger than they had been at birth. Obviously they had been getting little or no milk. Preparations were made one year to take a cub away from its mother and try hand rearing it, but all attempts to separate it failed. During this period, however, another pair of Kodiaks at Copenhagen Zoo produced a cub which was successfully reared by hand.

At last, however, success did come to Whipsnade. Two male cubs were born on 29th January 1954, and these the mother reared successfully. She did not take them out of the den into the pit until April 2nd, when they were nine weeks old. Subsequently other cubs have been reared at Whipsnade. A full-grown male

## Carnivores in Need of Protection

Kodiak bear standing on his hind legs reaches a height of more than ten feet, and his weight is not far short of a ton. The female is a little smaller. They do not, however, reach full size or complete maturity until they are between eight and ten years old, although they begin mating and producing cubs, at least in captivity, long before this. The story of the Chicago and Whipsnade pairs suggests that although the females may produce cubs while they are still growing, they cannot nourish them properly. An adequate flow of milk is possibly not produced until they become fully mature.

Little is known about how long bears may be expected to live, but there are records of ordinary brown bears living for well over forty years in captivity, and a solitary Kodiak bear lived for a similar length of time in the New York Zoo. There is every reason to hope, therefore, that the few pairs of Kodiak bears at present in captivity may be at the beginning of a long successful breeding career. The survival of the species may well depend eventually upon the maintenance of small breeding stocks in various zoos.

Second only in size among the world's carnivores to the Kodiak bear and the related large bears of Alaska is the polar bear (*Thalarctos maritimus*). Although it is still quite plentiful, its condition has been giving some anxiety in recent years, and the position needs to be watched carefully, because if certain present trends continue it could quite possibly become endangered before very long. Together with certain arctic animals, the polar bear plays a major part in the economy of the northern Eskimos, and its disappearance or serious depletion would be a matter of considerable concern to them.

Polar bears are widely distributed, but are naturally more plentiful in some areas than in others. They occur almost throughout arctic North America and also along the east and west coasts of Greenland, as well as in Spitzbergen and other extreme northern parts of Europe. They are essentially animals of the coast, where they occur among the pack ice, for nearly all their food comes from the sea. Biologically all bears are carnivores, but in their feeding habits the majority of species are omnivorous rather than carnivorous. The polar bear, however, is much more carnivorous than any of the others. It feeds principally on the harp seals which occur in large numbers everywhere in arctic waters, but it also eats other seals, fish, birds, and any carrion such as stranded whales which it comes across. The walrus is rather too powerful an animal to be tackled, but young ones separated from their mothers are considered fair game. Many instances have been recorded of dead polar bears having been discovered with extensive wounds, which appear to have been caused in a struggle with a full-grown walrus. In stalking seals hauled out on the ice the polar bears are of course greatly helped by their white or yellowish fur, which makes it extremely difficult for their victims to detect them until it is too late. They appear to be able to smell the carcase of a stranded whale from great distances away, and assemble to share the feast in considerable numbers, several dozen have been seen in the neighbourhood of a large specimen.

Opinions seem to differ about the ferocity of the polar bear. Some native hunters say that the polar bear will attack unprovoked, and there seem to be reliable examples of polar bears actually stalking a hunter among the ice floes. Others report that, except during the winter, when hunger perhaps makes them more bold, polar bears, like most wild animals, will make off for the nearest sea at the approach of a man. Both opinions may well be right. Those polar bears which have had some experience of man's aggressive intentions may understandably make every effort to keep out of his way. Others which have drifted into his vicinity on ice floes, from regions in which they have not come into contact with him, may well understand no reason to fear him, and are thus bold and aggressive.

To Eskimos of the northern coasts the polar bear, or nanook

as it is called, has always loomed large in their lives, figuring in their legends as well as contributing to their welfare. To kill a polar bear by the old method was a courageous and dangerous exploit. Using his dog team to bring the animal to bay, the Eskimo would close in on it and kill it with a long-handled lance, or if he was particularly brave, with a large knife. Today, of course, the Eskimos hunt with much greater safety using the rifle.

Almost every part of the polar bear could be used, the skin for bedding, clothing and sledge rugs, and the flesh for food. Although inclined to be somewhat stringy, the meat is apparently quite palatable. One curious fact about the polar bear is that its liver is poisonous, the reason being that it contains such high concentrations of vitamin A that anyone eating it gets vitamin poisoning.

Little is known about the breeding habits of polar bears, but they are probably similar to those already described for the Kodiak bear. During the late autumn the pregnant female prepares to go into hibernation for the winter, choosing an area where the ice has been heaped into great piles. Among the drifted snow she digs deeply, forming a snug den, the opening soon filling up with wind-swept snow. The snow, forming a perfect insulation, allows the bear's body heat to be retained, and the cubs are born into a dark warm world with a temperature which has been found to be as high as 86° F. Like all bear cubs they are extremely small at birth, which occurs towards the end of November or early in December. Until the following March mother and cubs remain in the den, probably in a state of semi-torpor, the cubs meantime suckling and growing, so that when they leave the den they are about two feet in length and weigh about 20 lb. As soon as they come out of hibernation the mother leads them to the sea, where she can find plenty of food for them. Throughout the first summer and the following winter they stay with her, but with the approach of their second summer she finally chases them off to fend for themselves, so that she can mate again and prepare for her next litter. She thus normally breeds in alternate years.

There is some difference of opinion about what the male bears do during the winter. Some authorities say that they also hole up, while others maintain that they remain active, hunting on the pack ice. Probably those bears living in areas where the sea freezes over completely do den up, because they would be hard put to it to find sufficient food, but those which live in areas where there is broken pack ice with some open water throughout the year may well remain active.

The extent to which the polar bear is protected varies in different regions. In Canada only Eskimos and Indians are allowed to hunt it and to sell the skins. This is of course understandable, because they rely to a certain extent upon it for their livelihood. At the same time it seems that whereas at one time the Eskimo only killed bears for his own use, today the majority of the skins he obtains are sold down south, and he only keeps about one in five for his own use. This suggests that he is now depleting the stocks at a much higher rate than is necessary for his own economy. One solution to this problem might be to continue to allow the Eskimo and the Indian to shoot polar bears for their own use, but to forbid the export of skins from their territory. At present the Canadian Eskimo is taking about 400 adult bears each year. In Greenland there has been a steady and serious decline in the polar-bear population over the past thirty years, and it seems that only a measure of protection can save this particular population. The Danish Government has recently established a close season lasting from the beginning of June until the end of October, during which time it is illegal to kill polar bears. In other parts of the arctic the establishment of military bases and meteorological stations in ever increasing numbers is beginning to constitute a growing threat to the polar bears, for hunting them is becoming a favourite form of recreation.

# Carnivores in Need of Protection

Provided, however, that the various authorities in whose territories the polar bear lives remain alive to the potential dangers threatening it, and are prepared to take the necessary measures in time, there is no reason why the polar bear should ever become extinct. If it does, it can only be through folly and neglect of responsibilities.

Equally important with the polar bear in the Eskimo economy is the walrus (*Odobenus rosmarus*). Also like the bear it is essentially an animal of the arctic seas and coasts, which has suffered considerably from over exploitation in modern times. With the seals and sea-lions the walrus forms a separate division of the carnivore family consisting of creatures which are remarkably adapted to life in water. In general structure it lies midway between these other two groups. Although most authorities prefer to regard the Atlantic walrus of the arctic regions of Europe and eastern North America and the Pacific walrus of the arctic regions of western North America and Russia as belonging to a single species, others regard them as two different species, naming the Pacific species *Odobenus divergens*.

Like the true seals the walrus has no external ears, but it resembles the eared seals or sea-lions in its ability to turn its hind flippers beneath its body when it comes out of the water, so that it is more mobile than the true seals whose flippers remain extended behind their bodies and cannot be used to assist their movements on land. The walrus is a very big animal, a full grown male approaching a ton in weight. The most prominent feature is the pair of large upper canine teeth which project straight downwards to form formidable tusks. Curiously, these are not primarily weapons, though they can of course be put to very effective use if the need arises, and as already mentioned they enable the walrus to hold its own even against the polar bear. Their principal function, however, is in feeding, for the walrus, despite its size, feeds almost entirely on various molluscs which are found in great abundance both on and buried in the sea bed in many areas where the sea is shallow. With its tusks the walrus is able to dig these buried shells out of the sea bed, when the strong whiskers are used to help in the process of shovelling them into its mouth.

As in the case of the polar bear, if the walrus only had to suffer the legitimate depredations of the Eskimos for their own use, its numbers would probably be unaffected, but the factors which make it valuable to the Eskimo also make it commercially valuable. Walrus hunting dates from very early times. It is known that the Vikings hunted them, and by the beginning of the seventeenth century walrus hunting had become a regular occupation. There are many references from these times of groups of ships catching 1,000 or more walruses in a voyage. The walrus was indeed a valuable animal, because besides the hide it provided oil from its blubber and ivory from its tusks. It was, too, an easy animal to catch, because it had to come in to comparatively shallow inshore water to feed.

Three centuries and more of intensive hunting have left their mark. The Atlantic walrus has now vanished from a considerable part of its original area of distribution, and the southernmost limits of its distribution both in European and in Canadian waters have receded several hundred miles northwards. The Danish Government have realized that only some kind of restriction on hunting can save the walrus from final extinction, and have done a good deal to control its exploitation in Greenland. In certain areas and at certain times of the year killing is prohibited, and such hunting as is allowed is confined to the Eskimo populations. Even for them there is an important rule to be obeyed. No walrus may be shot unless it is first harpooned. This is to prevent the waste which would be inevitable if shooting were allowed without this restriction, for many walruses killed would not be recovered. The Canadian Government is considering similar measures to conserve its dwindling stocks.

The Pacific walrus has suffered at least as seriously as the

Atlantic form, so that whereas at one time it was widespread and numerous almost everywhere from Alaska to Siberia, including all the island groups in the Bering Sea, it is now confined to small isolated areas on the mainland coasts and to a few of the smaller islands. Despite their importance to them the Eskimos have been extremely wasteful in their methods of catching the walruses, shooting them on the ice floes and losing a high proportion of those killed. On the Siberian coast there is evidence that the resident population has taken greater care with the walrus populations, waiting until the animals come ashore at the breeding season, and then limiting those taken to a figure which will not endanger the total population. Latest reports suggest that numbers here are steadily increasing. In view of the economic importance of the walrus it seems inconceivable that now the position is fully realized the necessary steps to conserve and increase the remaining populations will not be taken.

We must now turn from the arctic to the tropics to consider the state of the Asiatic lion. It is a curious fact that even today it is impossible to say how this Asiatic sub-species (*Panthera leo persica*) differs from the more familiar African lion (*Panthera leo*). Both varieties are certainly very similar, but until much more is known about the structure of the Asiatic form it is best to regard it as a sub-species of the more numerous African species. There is certainly considerable variation between individuals of both varieties, and it may well be that when adequate anatomical studies have been made on a sufficient number of wild specimens of the Asiatic lion it will be possible to define the fundamental differences between the two kinds. One reason for the present lack of precise information on this point is that most of the few specimens which have been examined by zoologists have been zoo specimens, and it is well known that lions which live for a considerable part of their lives in captivity become significantly modified in many structural features, and are therefore no longer reliable guides to the structure of the species to which they belong.

Two thousand and more years ago the Asiatic lion was widely distributed throughout southern Asia, and extended into some parts of southern Europe. Its last stronghold in Europe was probably Greece, and even here it was probably exterminated by A.D. 100. In 480 B.C. lions are recorded as attacking the baggage animals of Xerxes' army. After their extinction in Europe their range in Asia steadily contracted. In Syria, Palestine, Iraq and Arabia they were quite common at the time of Christ, and are mentioned about 130 times in the Bible. They apparently survived in this region for more than another thousand years, becoming finally exterminated at the time of the Crusades, except in a few remote parts of Arabia, where a few survivors are believed to have persisted until the early years of the present century.

After 1884 the lions survived in the Indian subcontinent only in the Kathiawar Peninsular. In that year the last lion was killed in Central India, where a small population had survived for some time. The main reason for the contraction of the lion's area of distribution was the increase in human population and occupation of land. As agriculture developed, so the lion had to be shot. Miliary forces played a big part in its extermination in many areas. Certainly in India army officers were responsible for killing large numbers of lions. During the time of the mutiny, for example, a Colonel George Acland Smith himself killed nearly 300. Besides being the victim of royalty, government officials and army officers, the lion had also to contend with the increased use of firearms by the farmer and the herdsman. It has sometimes been stated that the tiger has been responsible for the gradual disappearance of the lion, but this is probably not so. The two species occupy different habitats, the tiger being essentially an animal of the dense jungle, whereas the lion prefers open country.

The survival of the lion in the Kathiawar Peninsular was probably due to several factors. The people living there have very
strong feelings against taking the life of any wild animal, and it is
a rather isolated area. Despite its relatively small size, the peninsular was divided up into no fewer than 202 small states, each
with its own ruling prince or maharajah. The last stronghold of
the lions is in the Gir Forest, which occurs almost entirely in
the former state of Junagarh, and after 1884 the nawabs of this
state showed a commendable concern for the future of the lions.
In 1900 the nawab declared the lions protected, and it was
stated that the total population of lions at this time was not
more than two or three dozen. This figure seems to have been
a very clever piece of propaganda on the part of the nawab,
designed to dissuade visiting royalty and other persons of importance from seeking permission to shoot one. It seems likely
that the actual lion population at this time was about 100, and
that the nawab knew this. With protection the lions steadily
increased in number, and enabled the nawabs to give permission
for three lions to be killed each year without endangering the
survival of the species.

Today the number is probably around 300. Unfortunately
the wild life, on which one would expect the lions mainly to
feed, is not at all plentiful, and has been steadily decreasing over
the years. The reason for this has been that the area has been
heavily overgrazed by native cattle, which have left insufficient
food for the wildlife of the forest. In consequence the lions have
to rely almost entirely on these domestic cattle and water-
buffalo for their food. The herdsmen, however, show little concern about the lions' depredations of their herds. Since they
apparently do not kill any of their cattle themselves, the lions
probably do them a very good turn by keeping their numbers
down. But for them the herds would grow even faster, and the
state of overgrazing would become even more acute than it is.

It seems therefore that the Gir Forest lions and the herdsmen live at peace with each other, the herdsmen accepting their losses rather as a payment they must make for the privilege of using the lions' forest for grazing. The lions in their turn show little fear of man and no aggressive tendencies towards him. No man-eater has been known in the forest for the past fifty years.

The future survival of the Asiatic lion population in the Gir Forest will depend ultimately upon whether the numbers of domestic livestock grazing the forest can be controlled. If they continue to increase a time may well come when so much of the forest has been overgrazed and made unsuitable for the lions and other wildlife that their very existence is threatened. The general attitude of the Indian Government towards conservation since independence, however, has been so satisfactory that it is extremely likely that they will be determined to take the necessary steps to ensure the permanent survival of the Gir lions.

The problem, however, is more than mere prevention of killing. The ultimate safety of the species will depend upon striking a satisfactory balance between the amount of domestic livestock allowed in the forest and the number of lions it can support. Today it is clear that far too many cattle and buffalos are living there, and until these are substantially reduced in numbers the lions' habitat will continue to shrink and the number of lions the forest can support will gradually fall. Really effective control would also help to increase the numbers of wild game so that these could eventually provide the lions with the bulk of their food. At present they are so scarce that their contribution towards the feeding of the lions is negligible. The principal species in the forest are two kinds of deer, the axis and the sambar, three kinds of antelopes, the little chinkara gazelle, the four-horned antelope and the nilgai or blue bull, together with monkeys, porcupines, foxes, leopards and wild hogs. The lions would be interested mainly in the deer, antelopes and wild hogs. Only the latter are at all common now, and probably the only species eaten by the lions in any numbers.

There is considerable difference of opinion as to whether the leopard should be killed or preserved. Some argue that the leopards compete with the lions for food, and should therefore be at least reduced in numbers. Others, however, point out that they confine their attentions mainly to the smaller animals, especially the porcupines and monkeys, which are of no interest to the lions, and that therefore they help to control the numbers of these animals which are competing with the larger game for the limited amount of available plant food. Only a thorough ecological investigation of the forest will provide the final answer to this and the other problems involved.

# 13

## The Preservation of Rare Birds

*

Of the birds which are now in need of protection the kiwi is surely one of the most extraordinary species— a bird which cannot fly and can hardly see. Although it is the national emblem of its native New Zealand, most New Zealanders have never seen it in its native haunts, on account of its habits. It is a completely nocturnal bird, living well away from human habitation in dense forests. During the daytime it hides away in small caves or under fallen trees, coming out only at night to feed. In daylight it is practically blind, and there is some doubt whether it can see much better at night.

To make up for its lack of sight, however, it has a very strong bill, which is extremely sensitive both to touch and to smell, the two senses on which the bird relies for nearly all its activities. When it comes out to feed it walks along continually tapping the ground with the tip of its bill, much as a blind man taps the pavement with his stick. From time to time it sniffs loudly. It is searching for earthworms, which are almost the only thing that it eats. As soon as it has detected one the bill is plunged into the ground and it is dragged out. So accurate is the bird's method of detection that it seldom has to make a second attempt. The nostrils, unlike those of any other bird, are placed at the very tip of the bill, where of course they are of most use. Sometimes during the digging operations soil and sand particles get into them and have to be forcibly blown out when the bill is withdrawn.

The efficiency of a kiwi's sense of smell has been demonstrated by putting an earthworm on the ground in front of it and letting it crawl away, holding the bird until the worm has travelled several yards. On being released it begins its characteristic tapping and sniffing, following the path taken by the worm with the certainty of a bloodhound until it has caught up with it.

In earlier times kiwis were very plentiful, but through a variety of causes they have become rather scarce today. They used to be caught in large numbers for food, and of course their inability to fly or to see made them easy victims. The Maoris, too, used kiwi skins as an important part of their ceremonial dress. Even so they would probably have remained quite plentiful but for the white settlers. They brought with them cats, dogs and ferrets, and all of these found the kiwi easy prey. So the kiwi was faced with possible extinction, but in good time the New Zealand Government realized the danger, and declared it illegal to kill or to capture kiwis without special permit. Only rarely is permission given to export them, so they are very seldom seen in zoos.

A few years ago London Zoo did receive one, and a most popular exhibit it was. Its arrival, though, created quite a headache for the zoo-keepers, for several hundred worms had to be dug up every day to satisfy its very healthy appetite. They hoped they might be able to persuade it to change to some more easily obtainable food, but it proved extremely obstinate and would not look at anything else. After a time, much to the relief of the zoo gardeners, arrangements were made for regular supplies to be sent from a worm farm in the Ise of Arran.

Like the African ostrich, the South American rhea and the Australian emu, the kiwi is a true flightless bird. Its wings have become reduced to mere remnants which are quite useless for any purpose, and its feathers look more like rough hair. Its legs, however, are very strong, and it can give quite a powerful kick.

The kiwi's breeding habits are no less interesting and unusual than its other activities. Nesting sites are similar to those chosen for sleeping. To begin with only a few twigs are collected, and perhaps a certain amount of excavating may be undertaken. In these preliminary preparations both parents co-operate. The female then lays one egg, which is incredibly large, weighing usually a little under one pound, which is about one-fifth of her own weight. Having achieved this mighty effort she loses interest and wanders off, leaving it to the male to incubate the egg, a long process taking about seventy-five days. During this time he rarely leaves the nest, and consequently gets very little to eat, so that by the time the egg hatches he has lost about a third of his original weight.

His duties are by no means over when the young chick at last appears. Although it is fully feathered when hatched, it is not strong enough to leave the nest for a week or so. To keep it in, the male barricades the entrance with sticks and leaves. When he does finally take the chick out he cannot of course see it if it strays far away from him, but he can always keep in touch with it by his sense of smell. Almost as soon as it is out of the nest the young bird starts digging for worms, its bill being already quite strong. Until it is old enough to look after itself the male guards the chick jealously, attacking any other bird that comes within reach. If it is frightened it always runs to its father for protection, but will have nothing to do with its mother, threatening her with its beak if she approaches.

For some time now kiwis have been kept in captivity at the Hawke's Bay Acclimatization Society's game farm near Napier, where the curator, Mr. F. D. Robson, has been able to make a careful study of the bird's behaviour. Here, on 9th October 1946, the kiwi was bred in captivity for the first time, when a female chick was hatched. One of the many interesting observations that Mr. Robson has made is that although the female kiwi seems capable of laying only one egg at a time, she may produce another a month later, returning to the nest to deposit it with the first one. Occasionally a third, and even a fourth may follow, also at monthly intervals. Multiple laying seems rather tough on the male, because each succeeding egg laid after the first increases his incubation time by another month, so that it is possible for him to be continuously engaged on incubating eggs and training young chicks for as long as six months at a time.

How long kiwis live is not known for certain, but it is well over twenty years. Specimens have lived at Hawkes Bay as long as this, and are known to have been several years old when they arrived. They are five or six years old before they reach maturity and begin to breed.

There are five different types of kiwi, all much alike in size and appearance. The one most commonly seen in captivity is Mantell's kiwi, the only one to be found on North Island. South Island has three species, and the fifth lives on Stewart Island to the south of New Zealand. The name kiwi is derived from the bird's call, in which the first syllable is long and the second short.

Besides the kiwi New Zealand also has a rare mystery bird, the notornis. Its story begins with the discovery of some bones in 1847 by a government official, Mr. W. Mantell. These were identified by the great British zoologist Sir Richard Owen as belonging to a hitherto unknown bird. Since no living specimens had ever come to light it was assumed that this bird, like the moa, was already extinct. Two years later, however, Mantell had the good fortune to fall in with some hunters who had just killed a specimen. Ignorant of its rarity, they were in process of eating it, but Mantell managed to save the skin. Shortly afterwards some Maoris captured another, and this Mantell was also able to get hold of. These two—the first living specimens to be discovered—were sent to the British Museum.

## The Preservation of Rare Birds

After this brief appearance notornis vanished again, and nothing more was heard of it for thirty years. Then, in 1879, a third specimen turned up, caught by a rabbiter's dog at the edge of a lake. This one was also sent to London, where it was put up for sale and bought by the Dresden Museum for 100 guineas. Again notornis vanished, and again, nineteen years later, another solitary individual turned up. This time the New Zealand Government stepped in and bought it for £250 to prevent it going out of the country. It was given to the Dunedin Museum.

Clearly notornis was a rare bird. In half a century only four individuals had been found. Perhaps it was nearing extinction. This seemed more and more likely as years passed and the fifth specimen was awaited in vain. Occasional rumours, however, kept alive a faint hope that perhaps in some rugged and uninhabited part of New Zealand the flightless mystery bird might still survive.

Then in 1948, just half a century after its last appearance, when all hope had finally been abandoned, notornis was found again. This time, though, it was not a chance individual, but a small colony occupying a remote mountain valley in South Island. At once the New Zealand Government stepped in and accorded it complete protection with heavy penalties for anyone found in possession of the bird or its eggs. Naturalists are now busy studying for the first time the life and habits of one of the world's most elusive birds.

Another interesting story of animal discovery in modern times was that of a bird called the Congo peacock, pursued for more than twenty years by a distinguished American naturalist, Dr. James Chapin, whose only clue to its existence was a single feather. From 1909 until 1913 Dr. Chapin spent a good deal of time in the Belgian Congo studying bird life and collecting specimens for various American museums. Just before returning home in 1913 he made a collection of feathers, some of which came from a native headdress. Back in America it was an interesting exercise to sort out these feathers and decide what kind of bird each one came from. Identification of single feathers is not easy, but Dr. Chapin's expert knowledge enabled him to place every feather except one of those from the head-dress.

This became a mystery feather. Many times it was taken out to be examined, and each time it had to be put back again. Some day he hoped he might be able to solve the mystery. Meanwhile he began speculating on the unknown owner of the feather, and decided it was some kind of game bird, possibly a pheasant, which as yet remained undiscovered. This, as it turned out, was a remarkable piece of detective work, but Dr. Chapin had to wait until 1936 before his guess was confirmed in a rather unusual fashion.

During the 1930's he paid several further visits to the Belgian Congo, and became very friendly with Dr. Schouteden, director of the Congo Museum. One day in 1936 when Dr. Chapin called to see him it chanced that he had gone up to the top floor of the building. This was not a public part of the museum, but was used for storing all kinds of things, including surplus and unwanted specimens. It was obvious that these discards were of no particular interest, so Dr. Chapin paid them little attention as he searched for his friend.

Suddenly his attention was arrested, for there in a dusty discarded case he saw two birds, and one of them carried wing feathers which were identical in every way with the mystery feather he had cherished for twenty-three years. But here was another mystery. These two birds, one a male and the other a female, were described as Indian peacocks. As such it had long ago been decided that they had no place in the Congo Museum, which exhibited only animals of the Congo, and had therefore been relegated to the top floor as being of neither use nor interest.

But to Dr. Chapin, who knew his birds pretty well, they

presented a further puzzle. He was quite sure that, in spite of the name given to them, no such birds existed in India. Where, then, had they come from? At least he now knew that the bird from which his mystery feather had been taken definitely existed. He was particularly interested, too, to see that the birds were indeed pheasants, as he had decided long since on the strength of his single feather. Fortunately Dr. Schouteden was able to help by explaining how the museum obtained the birds, and between them they gradually unearthed the whole story.

In the early 1900's an unknown employee of the Kasai Company, which operated in the Congo, made a collection of local birds. These were duly mounted and labelled, and kept in the company's offices. In 1914 the company presented this collection to the Congo Museum. Most of the specimens were renovated and put on show, but not the so-called Indian pheasants.

The truth now dawned on Dr. Chapin. These birds must be Congo rarities which had been caught and mounted by the amateur bird collector nearly forty years ago, and had then been misnamed. Not realizing that he had brought a new species to light, the unknown collector had not reported his find. Since that time no other specimens had ever been caught by anyone competent to identify them as a new species.

If all this was true, and assuming the birds had not become extinct meanwhile, intensive search should reveal others. In the hope that other residents in the Congo might be able to help, Dr. Schouteden published details of the bird, together with an appeal for information, in the Bulletin of the Congo Zoological Club. A few correspondents did write in from various widely separated localities to say they thought they had seen the bird, and Dr. Chapin made a careful note of all this information.

There was no time this year to organize a search, but he returned in 1937, and with the help of a native hunter he was able to locate and shoot one or two specimens, but did not succeed in capturing one alive. Careful examination confirmed that the bird did belong to the pheasant tribe. He renamed it the Congo peacock.

Other commitments and the subsequent outbreak of war prevented Dr. Chapin from returning to the Belgian Congo. After the war, however, the New York Zoological Society organized a collecting expedition to the Congo, live specimens of the peacock being the principal objective. The expedition was a great success, and in 1948 the New York Zoo was able to put on public exhibition the first living specimens ever brought out of Africa.

No bird in recent years has received more attention than the American whooping crane (*Grus americana*). The struggle to save it from the very brink of extinction is still going on, and it is as yet too early to say whether it will be finally saved. It was in 1938 that the United States Fish and Wildlife Service really set about the task that must have seemed hopeless. In that year the only known survivors of the species were ten adult birds and four immature chicks.

At this time all that was known about the bird was that it spent the winter in a certain small area in Texas, and then migrated northwards to somewhere in Canada to breed. By 1940 the number of birds appearing in Texas had risen to twenty-one adults and five immature birds, and for the next ten years or so the numbers fluctuated around this total. In 1947 the wintering area in Texas was established as the Aransas National Wildlife Refuge, but protection could not be really effective until the breeding grounds had been located and placed under absolute protection. From 1945 onwards the U.S. and Canadian Governments co-operated in their attempts to preserve the crane, one of the largest birds in North America, and to locate its breeding grounds. In 1947, and again in 1948, attempts were made to follow the cranes by aeroplane as they migrated northwards in the spring, but in each year the birds were lost before they had reached their destination. Numerous reports were received from various parts of northern Canada that the cranes had been sighted, but it was not until 1953 that the breeding grounds were finally located, in the Wood Buffalo National Park in the Northwest Territory of Canada. Here the birds are now guarded as jealously on their breeding grounds as they are on their winter grounds in Texas, 2,500 miles to the south. The danger of being shot on migration, however, still remains, for despite the publicity given to them, there are still people prepared to shoot at them if they get the chance.

Despite all the efforts at preservation, however, it is still much too early to estimate whether the species will be saved, for the numbers are not increasing as fast as had been hoped. Even in 1958 only twenty-six adult birds were known to exist, and these produced only five chicks between them. Since the final preservation of the species may depend upon the maintenance of small breeding stocks in captivity, it is interesting to record what has been achieved so far in breeding whooping cranes in captivity. Obviously with such a small total wild population, very few individuals can be obtained for experiments in captive breeding. In 1940, however, an injured female was captured in Louisiana, and was handed over for safe keeping to the Audubon Park Zoo in New Orleans. Eventually a mate was obtained for her, and in 1945 two eggs were laid, of which one was hatched. The chick lived only for a few days, but the event was important because it was the first occasion on which a whooping crane had been hatched in captivity. No further eggs were hatched by this pair until 1956, when two eggs were laid and both hatched. Again, however, hopes were dashed when one chick died within a few days, and the other when it was only forty-five days old. Success, however, was at last achieved in 1957 when another two eggs were hatched and both chicks reared to maturity. Another chick was successfully reared in 1958. It seems likely, therefore, that if the position of the wild population deteriorates

G

it may be possible to preserve the species by means of captive breeding.

In the last few years reports from reliable observers have been received of whooping cranes having been sighted in positions which do not seem to fit in with the Aransas—Wood Buffalo Park population. If they are accurate reports, it seems possible that at least one other undiscovered flock may exist. This of course would increase the chances of the crane's survival. Besides granting the bird absolute protection, the Canadian Government also prohibits flying over the nesting area at heights of less than 2,000 feet, lest the sitting birds be disturbed, a wise precaution in the light of the disturbances caused to the nesting flamingoes in the West Indies, mentioned later in the chapter.

In the early years of this century the Americans awoke to the fact, too late, that they had allowed the passenger pigeon to be reduced to a state where its preservation from extinction had become impossible, and had only saved the American bison from extinction at the eleventh hour. In their new-found awareness of their responsibilities towards their natural heritage, they looked around anxiously at their other wildlife, in the hope that in future they might detect species in danger in time to do something about their preservation. And the first species which claimed their attention was the trumpeter swan (*Cygnus buccinator*). There are only two species of swan in North America, the trumpeter and the rather smaller whistling swan (*Cygnus columbianus*). The latter, being a very wary bird breeding only in the virtually uninhabited far north of the continent, has never been in danger of extinction.

In earlier times the trumpeter swan was common and widely distributed throughout western and central North America. It was the advance of civilization which finally reduced the swan to the point of danger. Many birds were shot in the pursuit of 'sport', and even more for commercial gain. Throughout the eighteenth and nineteenth centuries there was a large and growing market for swans' breast skins, and the first step in the effort to preserve the species was to impose a ban on this trade.

In recent times another unusual hazard has been discovered. In lakes where regular wildfowl shooting takes place considerable quantities of spent lead shot fall to the bottom of the lake, and when the swans dive to pick up the gravel and stones they require for the proper digestion of their food, they are liable to pick up some of these shot as well. Once in their gizzards they lead to gradual lead poisoning. Today the wildfowl management officers both in the United States and Canada frequently have to catch up sick birds and give them 'stomach pump' treatment to rid them of the poisonous lead, and then adminster antidotes. This lead poisoning is a factor which may well have an increasing effect on wildfowl in many parts of the world.

It was not until 1917 that the American and Canadian Governments agreed mutually to protect the surviving trumpeter-swan population. Exact estimates of the present population are difficult to obtain, for the swans are widely scattered. However, it seems that the species may well be out of danger. Reliable estimates give the total United States population at about 400 birds, and the Canadian population at about 700. Many of these are immature birds, however, because the trumpeter swan does not reach maturity until it is five years old. Most of the United States population are located in the Red Rocks Lake Refuge in Montana and in the Yellowstone Park in Wyoming. In Canada, however, the only known nesting area so far discovered is in Alberta. Where the rest of the Canadian swans nest has still to be discovered. A scattered population is in particular danger from local persecution, but everything possible is being done to educate the public in order to enlist their support in the conservation of the swans. Despite this, however, many must fall victim to the guns of those whose only interest in a rare bird is as a possible trophy. Both in the United States and in Canada wildlife guardians are on duty in the known breeding areas to prevent wanton destruction. In some of the wintering areas in Canada the birds are fed during severe weather, and holes are kept open in the ice to enable the birds to obtain at least some of their natural food. With a total population of about 1,000, and an increasing public awareness of its responsibilities towards nature conservation, it seems reasonable to hope that the trumpeter swan will escape the danger of extinction which threatened it in the earlier years of this century.

Towards the end of the 1930's it seemed probable that the Hawaiian goose or nene (*Branta sandvicensis*), a relative of the European Brent goose, was heading for extinction. Only a dozen or two individuals remained in the island of Hawaii, and there were none breeding in captivity. That the species now seems likely to be saved is due largely to breeding in captivity, though great efforts have also been made to preserve the bird and to encourage its maintenance in the wild state. During the war it was feared that the bird might have become extinct in the wild state, but in 1955 a flock of twenty-two was sighted, the first time for nearly twenty years that more than eight had been seen at one time.

The greatest problem in the protection of the Hawaiian goose was to provide a suitable habitat for its breeding, where it would be safe from interference by man and by its natural enemies. All of its former territory had become part of a single cattle ranch. Fortunately the owners of the ranch were sympathetic towards the efforts to preserve the goose, and have recently agreed to give game preservation rights to the Hawaiian Board of Agriculture and Forestry, who will assume responsibility for the preservation of the geese.

As a result of the efforts which have been made over the past two or three decades, the wild population on Hawaii has been steadily increasing. Latest reports put the total number now at about fifty. Even if the geese had become extinct in the wild state in recent years, by no means an improbable contingency, the species would probably nevertheless have been saved, for efforts to establish breeding stocks in captivity have been particularly successful.

In 1951 Mr. Peter Scott, director of the Wildfowl Trust, was sent one male and two females from Hawaii. These were taken to the Trust's grounds at Slimbridge in Gloucestershire, and proved remarkably successful. By 1958 the Slimbridge flock numbered seventy-three birds, which was considerably more than the total world population in the wild state. To guard against possible losses due to disease Mr. Scott had already sent pairs of geese to each of five other wildfowl centres in Holland, France, Switzerland, England and the United States, in the hope that they, too, would each be able to establish a breeding population. The ultimate hope of the Trust is that when sufficiently large numbers of birds exist in captivity it will be possible to return surplus birds to Hawaii for release in the wild state. Thus with a total world population of more than one hundred birds, compared with two dozen or so a little more than ten years ago, it seems reasonable to feel optimistic about the chances of ultimate survival of the species.

Another Pacific island bird which has claimed the attention of the conservationists in recent years is the Laysan teal (*Anas laysanensis*), a duck which is found in the wild state only in the tiny Pacific island of Laysan, some 1,000 miles to the west of Honolulu. An expedition which went to this island in 1911 could find only six specimens of this bird, and its imminent extinction seemed certain. Fortunately, however, although no efforts were made at this time to preserve it, the teal did enjoy freedom from human persecution, and was not overburdened with natural enemies, so that it was able to survive. For the next forty years or so only occasional reports of its struggle to survive were received, and these were not very encouraging. In 1923 20 ducks were counted, but in 1936 only 11 were seen. By 1950 the position seemed a little more encouraging, for in that year 26 adults and 7 young were counted.

Then, quite mysteriously, the teal began to multiply very rapidly. The first indication of this remarkable improvement was received in 1955, when the director of the Pacific Oceanic Fisheries Investigations paid a brief visit to Laysan and counted no fewer than 161 teal. Two years later the numbers had risen still further. There were in fact too many of them now to be counted accurately, but there were at least 580 adult birds.

This rapid increase brought its own anxieties. Such a large population would be extremely vulnerable to any outbreak of disease, which might wipe out the entire stock on the island. The only possible safeguard against such a contingency would be to build up stocks elsewhere, from which a new stock could be returned to Laysan in the event of such a catastrophe. Accordingly arrangements were made in 1958 for pairs of Laysan teal to be distributed to several zoological parks and wildfowl centres in America and also to the Wildfowl Trust. To this end eighteen pairs were caught and removed to Honolulu, where they were kept for acclimatization and adjustment to a captive existence for some time until they were distributed in 1959. Plans are also being made to release some pairs in other suitable small islands in the Hawaiian group in the hope that other wild populations may be established.

Another American bird hovering on the very brink of extinction is the ivory-billed woodpecker (*Campephilus principalis*). A large bird with a distinctive black, white and scarlet plumage and white bill, was at one time common in many parts of the United States, where it lived in dense hardwood forests in river valleys. Its food consisted mainly of wood-borers which it extracted from dead and dying trees. As civilization advanced and the forests were cut down, so the woodpecker's habitat became reduced. Today on the mainland of America it is believed to be extinct. The last living specimen to be seen was probably one recorded by a biologist of the Wildlife Service in northern Louisiana in 1944. In 1949 reports were received that a few of the birds had been discovered in a remote district in Florida, and shortly after the area was declared a sanctuary for the woodpecker. Unfortunately further investigation failed to confirm the existence of the woodpecker, though of course there is always a slight hope that a small colony may yet turn up.

In Cuba, however, there may still remain a few pairs of a closely related sub-species. There, as in the United States, forest clearing was responsible for the steady extermination of the ivory-billed woodpecker except in the one small area where it still survives. An investigation into the present status of these last survivors was made in 1956 on behalf of the International Council for Bird Preservation. The findings were rather discouraging. Only six pairs were located, and since then there has been severe fighting in the area during the civil war in Cuba, so that it is impossible to say whether the bird is still in existence today or not.

Yet another bird of the New World whose present position is causing anxiety is the rosy flamingo (*Phoenicopterus ruber*), also known as the American or West Indian flamingo. At one time this flamingo was present in very large numbers in many of the islands of the West Indies, but one by one its former nesting sites have been abandoned, and its total numbers have steadily declined. Man has been the principal cause of this gradual disappearance. Traditionally he has always organized expeditions to the breeding grounds to collect eggs, but so long as the number taken was carefully regulated so as not to place too great a burden on the flocks, the flamingos flourished. In modern times, however, there has been a tendency for too many eggs to be taken, so that not enough have been left to enable the birds to replace their natural losses by young birds.

This however has only been one factor in the flamingo's decline. It is a notoriously nervous bird, especially on its breeding grounds. At the slightest disturbance it will fly off the nest, and if the disturbance is at all prolonged it may abandon it altogether. For this reason the development of the aircraft has been disastrous for the birds. An aeroplane flying overhead creates something near to panic, and two or three low flights in fairly quick succession over the breeding grounds are sufficient to complete the break up of a season's nesting. Ten years ago a Society for the Protection of the Flamingo was formed in the Bahamas, and this has done much good work in trying to get the egg collectors to limit their take, and also to eliminate low-flying aircraft from the few remaining nesting sites during the breeding season. With the problem realized, and a society for the birds' preservation, there seems little excuse for allowing the decline in the flamingo population to go on.

Although not in such imminent danger, two other species of flamingo have been drastically reduced in numbers in recent times, and unless the present trend is arrested they will be on the danger list before long. They are the greater flamingo (*Phoenicopterus antiquorum*) of southern Europe, Africa and Asia, and *Phoenicoparrus jamesi*, which lives in the Andes. As with the rosy flamingo, persecution and disturbance are the twin causes of the serious decline in their numbers.

# 14

## The Island Survival of Primitive Reptiles

★

The giant tortoises are among the earth's oldest inhabitants. They date from a time long before the great Age of Reptiles, when the unwieldy dinosaurs and their numerous kin ruled the earth. Most of their contemporaries and many of their successors have long since become extinct, leaving only fossil records for evidence of their existence, but the tortoises still exist, though their position is far from secure. Having withstood the natural challenges of countless millions of years, they now face extinction at the hands of modern man.

Often the present-day distribution of an animal only makes sense if we know its remote history, and this is particularly true of the giant tortoises. They are now found only in two widely separated island groups, the Galapagos Islands situated in the Pacific Ocean some 500 miles off the coast of Ecuador, and in the Aldabra, Seychelles, and the Mascarene Island groups in the western Indian Ocean. In much earlier times, however, giant tortoises were widely distributed throughout many tropical and subtropical parts of the world. Here they succumbed in the course of time to various predators. That they survived in these island groups long enough for men to become acquainted with them is due to the fact that there were no predators. Consequently they were able to flourish to the limits of the available food supply. Despite their wide geographical separation, the histories of the two groups in the centuries following their discovery have been strangely parallel.

## The Island Survival of Primitive Reptiles

It was a bad day for the Galapagos tortoises when Fray Tomas de Berlanga, a Spanish explorer, discovered the Galapagos Islands in 1535. So numerous were the tortoises at this time that the islands were named after them, galapagos being the Spanish word for tortoise. They were soon found to be good to eat, and the Galapagos Islands became a regular port of call for mariners in the Pacific. Here they were able to replenish their water-barrels and their larders. Dampier, writing of the Galapagos Islands in 1697, tells us that 'the land turtles are so numerous that five or six hundred men might subsist on them alone for several months, without any other sort of provision. They are extraordinarily large and fat, and so sweet that no pullet eats more pleasantly.'

In the days before refrigerators and cold storage the tortoises had, unfortunately for themselves, one great advantage. Provided they were kept fairly cool and moist, and their shells were not damaged, they would live quite well for a year or more in a ship's hold without eating, and were therefore a perfect form of food to carry on a long voyage. The cook merely killed a tortoise whenever fresh meat was required.

Captain Porter, describing a call at the Galapagos Islands in the early days of the nineteenth century, tells us that 'in four days we had as many on board as would weigh about fourteen tons. They were piled up on the quarter-deck for a few days with an awning spread over to shield them from the sun, which renders them very restless, in order that they might have time to discharge the contents of their stomachs; after which they were stowed away below as you would stow any other provisions, and used as occasion required. No description of stock is so convenient for ships to take to sea as the tortoises of these islands. They require no provision or water for a year, nor is any further attention to them necessary than that their shells should be preserved unbroken.'

On the other side of the world, the Indian Ocean giant tortoises had been discovered at about the same time as those of the Galapagos Islands. Leguat, writing of the Island of Rodriguez in 1691, has recorded that 'there are such plenty of land turtles in this isle that sometimes you see two or three thousand of them in a flock, so that you may go above a hundred paces on their backs.'

Like their Galapagos cousins, they, too, were exploited for food without thought for their ultimate preservation. Some idea of the enormous numbers that went into the cooking-pot may be gained from the fact that in an eighteen-month period in 1759–60 no fewer than 30,000 tortoises were taken from Rodriguez alone. In another 100 years not a tortoise was to be found either on Rodriguez or on several of the other one-time heavily populated islands. Fortunately, though, large numbers still existed on Aldabra, and the folly of complete extermination was realized in the nick of time. Islands whose populations had been wiped out or seriously reduced were restocked from Aldabra, and indiscriminate slaughter forbidden. Farmers in the Seychelles Islands now keep many tortoises in a state of semi-domestication.

Originally each island had its own distinct species. Many of these were, of course, lost altogether, while the remainder have been crossed with each other through the movement from one island to another. As a result all the giant tortoises of the Indian Ocean are now classed as one species, *Testudo gigantea*, which, fortunately, seems quite safe from extinction.

All giant tortoises are strictly vegetarian, but whereas the Indian Ocean types had an abundance of available food, the Galapagos Islands are extremely dry and barren, many of them having no other water supply than that caught in temporary pools from irregular rainfall. Only a few of the larger islands have springs, and even these are located in the almost inaccessible interior regions, approachable only after an arduous trek across rocks and boulders. Succulent cacti and coarse grasses were therefore the only food available for the tortoises; the sharp spines of the cacti did not seem to bother them.

During the voyage of the *Beagle* Darwin visited the Galapagos Islands in 1835. Even then, after centuries of indiscriminate slaughter, the tortoises were still quite numerous. He was deeply impressed with the 'huge reptiles, surrounded by black larva, leafless shrubs, and large cacti that seemed to my fancy like some antediluvian animals'.

He goes on to describe their journey after water. 'The tortoise is very fond of water, drinking large quantities, and wallowing in the mud. The larger islands alone possess springs, and these are always situated towards the central parts, and at a considerable height. Therefore the tortoises which frequent the lower districts are obliged to travel from a long distance when thirsty. Hence, broad and well-beaten paths branch off in every direction from the wells down to the sea coasts; and the Spaniards, by following them up, first discovered the watering places. When I landed at Chatham Island, I could not imagine what animal travelled so methodically along well-chosen tracks. Near the springs it was a curious spectacle to behold many of these huge creatures, one set eagerly travelling onwards with outstretched necks, and another set returning after having drunk their fill. When the tortoise arrives at the spring, quite regardless of any spectator, he buries his head in the water above his eyes, and greedily swallows great mouthfuls, at the rate of about ten in a minute.'

Through the nineteenth century the Galapagos tortoises were less fortunate than those of the Indian Ocean. With no time to recover from the depredations of the seventeenth and eighteenth century mariners, they became the subject of a second type of exploitation. It was discovered that the fat from a full-grown tortoise could yield about three gallons of clear oil. Consequently, they were again slaughtered in their thousands in a wave of ruthless commercialism. For many years American whalers made a habit of calling at the islands on their way home and picking up as many as 300 tortoises at a time. Since there were several hundred whalers operating at this time, huge numbers must have been taken away over the years.

Darwin refers to the curious method adopted by these oil-hunters to find the best specimens for their purposes. 'When a tortoise is caught the man makes a slit in the skin near its tail, so as to see inside its body, whether the fat under the dorsal plate is thick. If it is not, the animal is liberated, and it is said to recover soon from this strange operation.'

By the end of the nineteenth century the tortoises had been completely wiped out of several of the islands, and since each island had its own particular species the loss was serious. In most of the other islands they were becoming rare. But worse was to follow. Although the animals were no longer killed either for food or for oil they still faced a third hazard, for which man was also responsible. He had unintentionally introduced rats, cats and dogs to the islands, escapees from his ships, and there were feral pigs on most of the islands descended from domesticated pigs which had been kept there at one time or another. With nothing to compete with these animals flourished, attacking the young tortoises, and digging out and eating the eggs which had been buried in the sand to hatch. Only the full-grown specimens were safe, and as these died off they were not replaced.

The position today is that the giant tortoises have certainly gone from at least two of the eleven islands that are known once to have had flourishing populations, and are probably also extinct on a third. On six others the numbers of survivors are so small that that there is little hope that they can be saved. Only on the two islands of Indefatigable and Albemarle are they still present in any numbers, and even here the rat and dog threat is very serious. The Albemarle population contains five distinct species.

## The Island Survival of Primitive Reptiles

Over the past thirty years the New York Zoological Society has been making great efforts to save the remaining Galapagos species. Transfer of specimens to other areas where conditions might be suitable for breeding seemed the only hope. There was no point in attempting to repopulate islands which had lost their tortoises, a policy that had been so successful with the Indian Ocean tortoises, because every one of the Galapagos Islands was overrun with predators. Other parts must be tried.

Accordingly, in 1928, the society sent an expedition to the Galapagos Islands to collect a breeding stock. One hundred and eighty specimens were brought home, and subsequently distributed in small groups to various scientific organizations in Bermuda, Honolulu, Arizona, Texas, Louisiana, Florida and Australia. The idea was a good one, but so far the successes have been very limited. In almost all of these areas the resident predators have proved too much for the young tortoises even when the climate has proved suitable for the eggs to hatch. It does seem that unless another area can be found which has both a suitable climate for hatching and an absence of predators, then the attempt will have to be abandoned. In 1960 Mr. R. Leveque, a U.N.E.S.C.O. observer who visited the Galapagos Islands, declared the position of the tortoises to be desperate. The only way of saving the remaining species, he suggested, was to set up a number of reserves on the islands, and to fence them completely round with barbed wire to keep out the various predatory enemies. Such barbed-wire sanctuaries would probably also be useful for preserving other Galapagos species which will probably need protection if they are to survive indefinitely. These include the flightless cormorant and the Galapagos penguin.

Giant tortoises live probably to well over 100 years, and when fully grown they are very heavy. Some years ago the London Zoo received what is believed to have been one of the largest specimens ever exhibited in captivity, and it turned the scales at over 600 lb. Large specimens, however, are not necessarily very old. The rate at which a reptile grows depends very much upon the temperature at which it is kept, provided that it is given plenty to eat. A young giant tortoise kept at the same sort of temperatures as it would enjoy in its native islands can reach giant size within twenty years from hatching. It will then go on growing, though more slowly, for the remainder of its life.

In the early years of this century rumours circulated in the East Indies that on one of the remote islands there lived an enormous dragon. Groups of adventurous native pearl fishers told convincing stories of a gigantic creature they claimed to have seen on the uninhabited island of Komodo, a tiny outlier of the Dutch Sunda Islands. This creature, they claimed, grew to more than twenty feet in length, and was as ferocious as you would expect a dragon to be.

Naturalists, however, were rather sceptical, feeling that if such a monster did really exist, then it would have been discovered long before. The natives, too, gave their alleged dragon a name which meant 'land crocodile'. It seemed likely therefore, that all they had seen were specimens of the estuarine crocodile, known to be widely distributed throughout the East.

Despite these doubts, however, Dr. P. A. Ouwens, a Dutch scientist working in Java, felt that the natives' claims ought to be investigated just in case they had found something new. Accordingly he arranged for a collector to visit Komodo Island to report on what he saw and, if possible, bring back some specimens. The result was perhaps a little disappointing, because he returned with four large lizards, which were similar, except in size, to a number of monitor lizards found in other parts of the world. They were, however, larger than any known monitor, and therefore the largest lizards in the world. The biggest specimen was about nine feet in length. This did not of course disprove the earlier claims for the size of the Komodo dragon, as it now came to be called, for these could well have been only small specimens.

Before further expeditions could be organized to continue investigations the First World War broke out, and the Komodo dragon mystery remained only partly solved. It was not until 1923 that further attempts were made to solve the problem, when the Duke of Mecklenburg went to Komodo and secured another four specimens, none of which, however, exceeded ten feet in length.

Claims that the Komodo dragon might attain a length of twenty feet might now have been discredited, but for the persistence of rumours. One story, for instance, told how a captive dragon burst its bonds and attacked a full grown horse, causing such injuries that it had to be destroyed, a feat well beyond the capacity of a ten-foot lizard.

It was not until the 1930's that the Komodo riddle was finally solved by an American expedition which visited the island to measure specimens and report on their mode of life. Their findings showed clearly that ten feet was the absolute maximum length for the male lizards, the females being two or three feet shorter.

What kind of animal is the Komodo dragon? Although in size it does not come up to its rumoured reputation, yet it is still a very large lizard, much larger and heavier than any other living lizard. On its native Komodo Island it lives in woods and on open grassland, especially on mountain slopes. And, true to its reputation as a dragon, it is ferocious and has a very healthy appetite.

Its diet is varied, and it will eat any living thing that it can catch, relying on its keen eyesight and sense of smell to locate its victims. Like the snakes, it has a forked tongue which is waved about to 'taste' its surroundings when it is on the prowl. Smaller specimens live on rats, mice, smaller lizards, insects, birds and their eggs, all of which are generally swallowed whole, but the giants go in for larger prey. Full-grown specimens are able to kill deer and wild boar. These they tear to pieces in the most ungainly fashion using their enormously powerful claws and teeth. Their capacity for swallowing really large joints is quite remarkable, a large dragon being capable of swallowing the complete hind quarters of a deer in a series of powerful gulps.

Whenever a rare and interesting animal is discovered there is always a danger that it will be hunted out of existence for some reason or other. In the 1920's lizard-skin handbags and purses were the height of fashion, and the Dutch Government was quick to realize that sooner or later someone would get the bright idea of turning Komodo dragons into leather goods. Consequently they decided to step in first, and in 1926 they issued an order prohibiting the taking of Komodo dragons alive or dead without a permit. These permits were only to be issued for scientific purposes to museums and zoos.

One of the first bodies to be granted a permit was London Zoo, and in June 1927 two specimens arrived there and created great public interest. They were put into a specially constructed den in the reptile house, where they basked in artificial sunlight at a temperature of 80° F. They proved easy to keep and became very tame, and even seemed to become attached to their keepers, a rare thing with reptiles, which generally seem quite impersonal. When they first arrived they were about seven feet long, and slim and agile like other large monitor lizards. As they grew, however, they became much heavier and bulkier, and less like their smaller cousins. Despite the great increase in weight, increase in length was very slow. After seven years the larger one had grown to just nine feet.

The Komodo dragon (*Varanus komodoensis*), is a survival from very remote times, when other lizards as large as and even larger existed. Several million years ago another lizard similar in size and structure to the Komodo dragon lived in Australia.

## The Island Survival of Primitive Reptiles

Presumably these large lizards died out in competition with other forms of life, the Komodo dragon being able to survive because no predators capable of dealing with it reached this particular island. The Komodo dragon may well be a direct descendent of the Australian form which managed to cross the seas from Australia to the East Indies. All monitor lizards can swim quite well, and were probably able to spread by island hopping, using the strong easterly current which flows through the Torres Straits.

# 15

# The Chinchilla and the Golden Hamster

★

High up on the bare slopes of the Andes lives a small rodent which boasts the most beautiful and the softest fur of any mammal. It is the chinchilla (*Chinchilla laniger*). It was first discovered by an Indian tribe, the Chinchas, more than a thousand years ago, and it was from them that it derived its name. They were quick to realize that its fur made ideal wear in the intense cold of the high mountain slopes, and it had the advantage of being as durable as it was warm.

Some centuries later the Chinchas were conquered by the Incas, another Indian tribe, and they in their turn appreciated the value of chinchilla fur. In addition to providing them with warm winter garments, the chinchilla fur was also adopted for ceremonial robes. The remarkable fur of the chinchilla was first introduced to Europe by the Spaniards, who invaded South America in 1542, conquering the Incas and learning about the wonderful fur of the chinchillas from them. With the jewels and precious metals which the Spaniards shipped back to their own country they also included some of the pelts of the little rodent. Immediately there was a great demand for it from the members of the Court, and from them the other Courts of Europe were soon made aware of it.

In order to preserve it for their own use, the royal houses of Europe soon passed laws forbidding any commoner to wear chinchilla's fur, so that it became known as the royal fur. For

350 years the trappings of chinchillas in the Andes to satisfy the demands of European aristocracy continued, and for a long time the little rodents seemed to survive despite the heavy annual toll. Towrdas the end of the nineteenth century, however, the continual drain began to tell, and the chinchilla was becoming scarce. Some idea of the toll taken at this time may be gained from the fact that in 1894 the exports of chinchilla pelts from Chile alone totalled more than 400,000, and similar numbers were trapped and exported from Bolivia and Peru.

Just in time the governments of these three countries realized that the animal was fast approaching extinction, and that something must be done quickly if it was not to be wiped out of existence. Accordingly they agreed to prohibit all trapping, and declared the export of pelts to be illegal. And so it was that the supply of chinchilla pelts to the fur markets of the world came to an end.

Chinchilla fur is extremely soft, and so light in weight that it is hardly heavier than thick silk. The softness is due to the fact that each hair is divided into some fifty hairlets as it leaves the hair follicle. Yet despite its fineness chinchilla fur is extremely hard wearing. The colour of the pelt is light grey shading somewhat darker along the back. To make a full-length coat about 300 pelts are needed, and these of course have to be very carefully matched.

Chinchillas in the wild state occur only in certain parts of the Andes, where they range between heights of 5,000 and 15,000 feet above sea level, where there is little vegetation or natural cover other than piles of loose rocks and rock crevices. Until it was brought almost to the verge of extinction by over-exploitation by man, the chinchilla flourished, and there must have been enormous numbers of them. Against its natural enemies its nocturnal habits must have been of great value to it. During the day it lies up, coming out of hiding to feed only after darkness has fallen. The only food available for it is the rather parched coarse plant life of the mountain slopes, but its requirements are modest, and it seems to thrive on a very meagre and relatively poor quality diet, a factor which has made it an extremely economical animal to maintain in captivity. To deal with its food it has strong teeth, which it sharpens on the volcanic pumice stone which forms much of the loose rock on the mountains. To keep its fur clean it takes dust baths in the volcanic dust. Its fur, however, is so thick that no vermin can live in it.

The rabbit breeders have produced a type which they call the chinchilla rabbit. Its fur certainly bears a resemblance to that of the chinchilla so far as its colouring is concerned, but of course it lacks the quality of the original. The chinchilla is not in fact at all closely related to the rabbit. It is a true rodent, related to the guinea-pig, while the rabbit is a lagomorph.

The virtual disappearance of chinchilla pelts from the fur markets of the world gave added impetus to the production and trapping of other high-grade fur-bearing mammals. Fox and mink ranching became big business. So successful was the breeding of mink in captivity that an American mining engineer named Matthias Chapman conceived the idea of ranching chinchillas in the same way. Chapman had been working in the Andes after the First World War, and there he came into contact with the now rare wild chinchilla. In spite of the ban on their capture and export, he managed to get permission from the Chilean Government to take a few pairs back to America with him in 1923. His efforts were phenomenally successful. The little creatures proved both hardy and prolific in captivity, and were extremely easy to feed and keep in good health.

It was not long before chinchilla farms were being set up all over the United States, and a little later the enterprise spread to Canada as well. By the end of the Second World War chinchilla breeding had become an important industry. Millions of chinchillas had been bred from the few original pairs.

## The Chinchilla and the Golden Hamster

As captive animals chinchillas have many advantages over mink. They are friendly creatures, entirely without smell, and their vegetarian food costs about £1 a head annually. Their poor diet in the natural state makes their requirements in captive very frugal. In fact rich food must be avoided, and too much fresh green food can be dangerous. Like many other rodents their rate of increase is rapid. Each pair may produce two or even three litters in a year, each litter containing on an average two young. The gestation period of about 110 days is extremely long for so small an animal, but the young are active and fully able to fend for themselves as soon as they are born. This is presumably an adaptation to their life on the mountains, where a prolonged infancy dependent upon their mothers would not be safe. To compensate for the very long gestation period the female will often mate again within twelve hours of giving birth to a litter.

In captivity chinchillas usually rest during the day, becoming lively towards evening, when they have their one meal of the day. They must have their daily dust bath, and this is given before they have their meal. Fuller's earth has been found to be the best substitute for the natural volcanic dust. In their cages small pieces of pumice stone provide them with the means of sharpening their teeth.

Chinchillas are normally so rotund that it is impossible to tell from her appearance when a female is pregnant, but her behaviour usually gives her away. Captive chinchillas are almost always very affectionate towards those who look after them, but during the few weeks before she is due to give birth to a litter the female chinchilla becomes even more gentle and dependent.

When myxomatosis first appeared in Britain the chinchilla breeders became very anxious lest the disease could affect their stocks. Experimental injection of the virus to a number of chinchillas failed to show the slightest signs of susceptibility, nor did they show any signs of being able to contract distemper. So far, indeed, no one has found any disease to which they are susceptible.

While the vast majority of chinchillas alive today are in captivity, the total world population of another small rodent is, so far as we know, living in this state. It is the golden hamster (*Cricetus auratus*). The species was first discovered in the desert near Aleppo in Syria in 1930. Thirteen specimens were found there, and a few of them were brought back to Europe with the aim of studying their biology and determining their exact classification. It was not difficult for the zoologists to decide that they were closely related to the somewhat larger European hamster, which is found in most parts of central Europe.

The golden hamster, as it was called, proved very easy to breed in captivity, and had a docile and friendly disposition which made it an excellent pet. It was easy to feed and easy to breed. Within ten years it had become extremely popular both in Europe and in many other parts of the world where it had subsequently been introduced. It is, however, something of a mystery, because since the discovery of the thirteen individuals more than thirty years ago, not a single additional wild specimen has ever been found, either in Syria or anywhere else. It seems possible therefore that these original specimens may have been among the last remnants of a species on the very verge of extinction in the wild state. But for the lucky discovery in 1930 it may well have become extinct without ever having been discovered. Of course, another colony may be discovered at some future date, but meanwhile the known world population today consists of many thousands of captive specimens.

Besides the chinchilla there are two other South American mammals which are in danger of extinction, the red or maned wolf (*Chrysocyon brachyurus*) and the paca-rana (*Dinomys branickii*). Neither species, however, owes its present precarious position to presecution by man, for both were quite rare animals when they were first discovered. The common name of the maned wolf is not really a very satisfactory one, since the animal has no pronounced mane and it is not a wolf. It is in fact a kind of wild dog about the size of a wolf with very long legs and long ears. Unlike the true wolves, too, it is a solitary species, and never goes about in packs. Its food consists of small animals such as rodents, birds, reptiles and insects, and it is not a danger either to man or to any large animals, though the occasional individual may attack sheep. It occurs in Brazil, Paraguay and northern Argentina, but even in areas where it is known to exist it is very seldom seen because of its nocturnal habits. During the day it lies up in dense undergrowth, coming out only after darkness has fallen to feed. Since the maned wolf is not persecuted by man, there seems little or nothing that can be done to ensure its continued survival. If it does finally become extinct this will therefore probably be from natural causes over which man can have no control.

South America is very well stocked with medium and large rodents, and the paca-rana is one of these. It is something like a guinea-pig or an agouti in appearance, and it is related to these two common rodents of South America, but it is rather larger. Full grown paca-ranas are some two feet in length, and their fur is brown decorated with longitudinal rows of light spots. Like the agoutis they are nocturnal animals which feed on plants. There seems to be some doubt today whether the species is already extinct or not, but in Peru there are plenty of areas where it might well still survive unknown to man. As with the maned wolf, there is little that can be done to help its survival in any case.

Another South American mammal whose present status is causing anxiety is the guanaco. At one time it was numbered in its millions in Argentina, Bolivia, Chile and Peru. Related to the llama, itself a member of the camel tribe, it is essentially an animal of the semi-desert country of the mountain areas, where it ranges from sea level up to 13,000 feet. Guanacos, or huanacos as they are called in Chile and Perus, live in small herds each consisting of up to ten females led by a single male. Young males without a harem unite in larger herds up to fifty.

Exploitation of the guanacos has been going on for several centuries. When the Spaniards conquered South America they began killing the guanacos in large numbers to feed their troops, but despite fairly continuous persecution right up to the end of the nineteenth century, their numbers remained high. In the sixteenth century there were probably several million of them, and at the end of the nineteenth century several hundred thousand probably still remained. Two factors, however, were responsible for a sudden increase in exploitation from the beginning of the present century. There was at this time a big increase in the demand for the pelts of the guanaquito, as the young guanaco is called, and at the same time the native Indian population obtained plentiful supplies of firearms, which made it easy for them to meet these increased demands. As sheep and cattle ranching increased, so the farmers killed the guanacos on the grounds that they competed with their stocks for the available food supplies. In area after area the guanaco has been systematically exterminated.

There is one curious aspect of this exploitation. Since it is mainly the young which are killed, the adults go unmolested, so for many years the adult population remains fairly constant. But when these come to the end of their thirty or so years of life and begin to die off there is a sudden collapse in the population because none of the intervening age groups have survived to replace them. The threat to a species by the killing of the young rather than of the adults is unusual.

Although during the past two or three decades attempts have been made to protect the remaining populations of guanacos by legislation, the four countries concerned have unfortunately not co-ordinated their efforts, and so have left loopholes for the unscrupulous. The only permanent hope for the guanacos seems to lie in the establishment of properly safeguarded reserves.

# 16

## *Australia's Danger Species*

\*

Although Port Jackson, near Sydney, was discovered and named by Capt. Cook, no white man settled there until 1788, when a small colony was founded. Ten years later a young man from this colony set off inland in order to find out something about the land behind the port. On this journey he was destined to discover one of Australia's most delightful animals. Most people who have made important animal discoveries in modern times have left us their names, but of this young man we know neither his name nor anything about him.

After travelling some sixty miles he reached the Blue Mountains, and here he came across a most attractive sight. Sitting in the trees were great numbers of tiny bear-like creatures with large heads, big furry ears, and prominent noses looking for all the world like blobs of black rubber stuck in the middle of their rather humorous-looking faces. The Australian natives called them koalas, so to the white settlers they became koala bears.

Like all Australian mammals, the koala bear is a marsupial or pouched mammal, and not at all related to the real bears. Its young are born at a very early stage of development, which is completed in the pouch. Even when the well-developed young finally emerges after spending several months in the pouch, it still stays with its mother, riding on her back, until it is about a year old.

It is a curious fact that a healthy koala bear never drinks. Only a dying specimen has ever been seen to take water. Nor is it capable of sweating. In hot weather it will lick its fur, cooling being effected by the evaporation of the saliva. One result of the lack of sweat is that the animal always smells very sweet, the only odour being that of eucalyptus from the leaves of which it feeds.

In modern times one of the biggest handicaps to any animal is the possession of a warm and durable fur, and the koala bear has been one of these sufferers. For many years koala bears were hunted for their fur. Killing reached a peak after the First World War, when in a period of two years more than 200,000 paid the penalty. Certainly koala fur is attractive, warm and hard wearing, but you can no longer buy a koala coat. After the little creature had become exterminated from large areas of Australia, the government intervened and banned large-scale exploitation. Today great care is taken of those that remain. It would indeed have been a grave reflection on civilized man had he allowed such a delightful creature to join the ranks of the many other animals that his greed and folly have wiped off the face of the earth.

There is one very disappointing thing about the koala bear. It is the kind of animal the public would adore, yet it has proved impossible to keep it in zoos for any length of time, even in its native Australia. For years the reason for this was surrounded in mystery. One difficulty was that it would eat only the leaves of eucalyptus trees, or gum trees as the Australians call them, which made it useless to attempt to keep it except in places where fresh daily supplies of eucalyptus leaves could be provided.

This, however, was not the complete answer. In Australian zoos ample supplies of these leaves were available for the picking, but always the results were the same. A batch of captive koalas would live quite happily, perhaps for as long as eight or nine months, and then within a period of days or weeks they would all die. Post-mortem examinations gave no clue as to the cause of death, for there were never any signs of disease.

Recently, however, the mystery was solved by Ambrose Pratt, President of the Royal Zoological Society of Victoria. He was struck by the fact that death was always sudden, an animal being perfectly fit one day and dead the next. This suggested that death was caused by acute poisoning. He remembered, too, an occasion when seventeen koalas were brought to his zoo. Three of them escaped after a short time and took up residence in a eucalyptus tree in the grounds of the zoo, where they could be kept under observation. The fourteen which remained in captivity all died after a few months, but those that had escaped remained in their tree for three years. Then they were re-captured, only to die a few months later.

During their years of freedom, however, Ambrose Pratt saw something which made him think. Up in the tree the three koalas seemed nearly always to choose old tough leaves instead of the juicy young leaves at the tips of the branches. In the zoo koalas were always fed on young leaves in the belief that these would be the most nourishing. Could it be that young eucalyptus leaves contained a poison which disappeared as they got older?

It was now that Pratt decided to find out what the botanists could tell him about the eucalyptus leaves. All his speculations about poisoning seemed much more likely to be true when he was told that the young leaves of the sugar gum, one of Australia's two hundred-odd kinds of eucalyptus trees, did in fact produce the deadly poison prussic acid during a certain period of their development. Later, as they grew older, the prussic acid disappeared, and the leaves were no longer poisonous.

Encouraging though this news was, there was one snag. Koalas were only interested in, and would only eat, the leaves of about five kinds of gum trees, and the sugar gum was not one of these. Unaware of Pratt's speculations, however, a group of Australian botanists had been carrying out further investigations into the production of prussic acid in the leaves of other kinds of eucalyptus trees, and they found that the leaves of most varieties, including those eaten by the koalas, produced prussic acid during their period of development.

The answer to the koala mystery was now obvious. Left to their own devices, koalas always chose the older harmless leaves, whereas in the zoo they had to eat the poisonous young leaves or starve, because no one thought of offering them older leaves that would do them no harm. Given an adequate choice of old leaves they could now be kept in captivity without fear of sudden death. As zoo animals, though, they must still be mainly confined to Australia, for only there do their favourite gum trees grow.

Most people seeing koala bears for the first time are struck by their resemblance to teddy bears. This is not surprising because the man who made the first teddy bear modelled it on a stuffed specimen of a koala bear, and named it after the famous American President, Teddy Roosevelt, who was also a distinguished hunter and naturalist.

One of the most interesting features of the Australian fauna is that in the absence of higher placental mammals the marsupial or pouched mammals have undergone a series of parallel evolutions to produce animals occupying the same ecological niches as placental mammals in other parts of the world. Often, too, the ecologically similar types have evolved similar structural features. Thus in the absence of deer, cattle and antelopes, the kangaroos and wallabies have become Australia's grazers.

Perhaps the most remarkable of these examples of parallel evolution is the Tasmanian wolf (*Thylacinus cyanocephalus*), the most perfectly adapted Australasian carnivore. Not only does it resemble the true wolf in general size and appearance, but its skull and teeth are so similar to those of the wolf that on superficial examination they are indistinguishable. It has, however, prominent chocolate-coloured stripes running transversely across the back. It was at one time widely distributed on the mainland of Australia, but is now confined to Tasmania. Its disappearance from the mainland was probably due at least in part to the introduction of the dingo by the early white settlers. It was, however, like the true wolf, an extremely ferocious animal, and proved very destructive to the sheep, so that the farmers invariably shot it on sight. In Tasmania it survives mainly in remote mountain glens where it can hide away in the daytime in caves and rock clefts, coming out only after dark to hunt. With care it should be possible to save this last remnant of the population from final extinction.

Although physically as well equipped as the true wolf, the Tasmanian wolf seems to lack its intelligence and cunning, and this may of course have played an important part in its extermination. Sir Ray Lankester, the distinguished British zoologist, observed that, 'when one watches the Tasmanian wolf, one comes to the conclusion that it is stupid and of much lower intelligence than the common wolf. Its appearance, ways, and movements suggest the fancy that it is a kangaroo masquerading as a wolf, and not very successful in the part.'

In addition to its well-known animals, Australia also has a mystery animal. Nearly 100 years have passed since the Australian tiger-cat was first described, but even today no one knows whether it really exists. Have all the people who at various times since then have claimed to have seen it been the victims of an illusion, or is there still lurking undiscovered in the vast unexplored forests of northern Australia some large cat-like animal that will one day be brought to light and perhaps exhibited in the zoos of the world for all to see? The question whether the tiger-cat is fact or fiction is certainly an intriguing problem.

Science first heard about these tiger-cats in 1871, when a Queensland magistrate wrote to the secretary of the Zoological Society of London describing an encounter his thirteen-year-old son had had with one of them. One evening the boy was strolling along the shore with his terrier, when the dog suddenly became very excited, barking furiously and making its way inland through tall grass, obviously following a strong scent. The boy followed the dog as fast as he could for about half a mile before catching up with it. It had stopped a yard or two from another animal which had been resting in the grass, and was barking defiantly.

Although the boy was only young, his knowledge of the bush and its animals was better than that of many adults. And he knew at once that this animal was something unusual. 'Its face was round like that of a cat,' he told his father afterwards. 'It had a long tail, and its body was striped from the ribs under the belly with yellow and black. My dog flew at it, but it could throw him. When they were together I fired my pistol at its head; the blood came. The animal then ran up a leaning tree, and the dog barked at it. It then got savage and rushed down the tree at the dog and then at me. I got frightened and came home.'

The father was extremely interested in what his son had told him, and during the following weeks made many inquiries in the neighbourhood. He learned that others besides his son had caught glimpses of a similar unknown animal. Unfortunately no one had ever managed either to shoot or capture a specimen. A year later the Zoological Society received another letter from the same part of Queensland describing how a party of engineers out on a survey were disturbed one evening by a loud roar just outside their tent. They seized their guns and made a careful search, but found nothing. Next morning, however, they found the tracks of their mysterious visitor, and were able to make careful drawings of its footprints.

The existence of the tiger-cat seemed established beyond reasonable doubt, and it could only be a matter of time before a specimen would be available for the experts to examine, or so it seemed at the time. Yet despite the fact that over the next twenty or thirty years it was reported in various parts of Queensland on a number of occasions, somehow it still managed to elude capture or death.

The position today is that no claims to have seen the tiger-cat have been made for a good many years. Does this mean that zoologists have begun to disbelieve in its existence? Not entirely, but of course the hopes that a new and particularly interesting animal will sometimes be added to the Australian list are not as bright as they were at one time. On the other hand it must be remembered that in that part of Australia there are still vast tracts of virtually unexplored bush, where a shy and stealthy animal might well have escaped discovery over all these years.

## Fauna Preservation and the Future

\*

The main purpose of this book has been to examine the whole problem of fauna preservation in the light of what has been achieved to date. Inevitably, however, the question of the future must arise, and although this is not the place for an exhaustive survey of the probable turn of events, some forecast of what is likely to happen seems desirable.

In countries where government-sponsored wildlife protection organizations are well established the future seems bright. It is about the wildlife of those parts of the world where there is a great deal of political instability that the conservationist feels despondent, because any drastic change in political control may well result in the destruction of such measures for fauna preservation as are at present in existence or are being developed.

Before India gained her independence after the last war fears were expressed for the future of her quite rich array of rare wildlife. It was felt that the new governments might well identify wildlife conservation and the sanctuaries which had been established with the retiring white rulers, and persuade their people that these must be abolished, along with so much else which belonged to the white raj. In the event the pessimists were confounded. The new governments, and especially that of India, regarded the conservation of wildlife almost as a matter of national pride, and far from trying to curtail the work done in the existing reserves, they gave it renewed encouragement, and have subsequently set up additional reserves.

Although there will of course be many more battles to be fought for individual species, it seems certain that the attempt to conserve what remains of our fauna will receive increasing support both from governments and from the public, so that the danger of extinction for most rare species is less today than it was a few decades ago, and should continue to diminish. There is, however, no room for complacency. Continued vigilance against the efforts of vested interests by preservation societies will still be necessary.

It is with the future in Africa that there is cause for grave concern. With the exception of South Africa, where there is a long tradition of conservation, and the world's finest national park, the possibility of large-scale destruction of wildlife seems to be very great. Over the past few decades great efforts have been made to set up and develop game reserves in almost every one of the countries south of the Sahara. But these have been achievements of white governments often against determined opposition. This has come in the main from the native populations. Now we are faced with perhaps almost the whole of Africa except South Africa being handed over country by country to the Africans.

To the majority of Africans the animal life of their countries means food. They seem to have little appreciation of the ecological or any other value which might attach to their very rich fauna. Nor, it seems likely, will they be able to understand and accept the results of ecological surveys which have recently shown how disastrous continued reduction in the wildlife and increase in the native cattle would be.

As a result of these surveys strong recommendations have been made concerning the balance between wildlife and cattle. Native cattle are extremely inefficient judged by the amount of food they produce, one reason being that far more are kept in

226

most areas than the area can really support. Also because their grazing is selective, the land on which they live becomes progressively poorer, so that it can support less cattle and fewer wild animals. If the number of cattle was drastically reduced and the antelope populations allowed to increase, then it has been shown that a given territory could yield a much greater annual weight of antelope meat than it does beef, and the meat would be of much better quality. To the African, though, the importance of his cattle lies in the prestige which they confer, and not in the economic value of their meat.

Thus to ensure adequate protection of African wildlife a great deal has to be done in a very short time. Firstly the African must be convinced of the cultural and educational value of maintaining representatives of every species, even if only in national parks and nature reserves. Also he will have to realize that protection is an active and not a passive resolve. One of the great problems which conservationists have to face in Africa today is the poacher, who takes an enormous annual toll of all economically important animals. But to the majority of Africans the poacher is doing no wrong. He is merely using animals for their one rightful purpose, economic exploitation. The African ruler, even supposing he wants to, will find it extremely difficult to mobilize public opinion against poaching, and if he cannot get this support he will find it very hard to maintain effective conservation. The third lesson the African will have to absorb is that properly controlled economic exploitation of game animals, outside such reserves as he may decide to retain, could bring a considerable improvement in the native diet by providing more meat than he can ever hope to obtain from his native cattle, but that to achieve this he must face a very drastic reduction in the number of cattle he can keep.

The best hope for the future of what is the most spectacular mammal fauna in the world is probably for a concentrated joint effort by U.N.E.S.C.O., the International Union for the Conservation of Nature, the Fauna Preservation Society, and the various preservation bodies already existing in Africa, to convince the educated African of the value of these ideas. If financial aid is required initially to help the change in economic habits, this should of course be forthcoming.

Meantime if everyone who feels that conservation is a worthwhile aim would join whatever body exists in his country, then he will be helping to further the work of conservation in all parts of the world, for conservationists are now organized and working on a completely international basis, as has been made clear in this book.

# Index

# Index

# Index

# Index

*Vanishing Animals*